100 BEST

FAVORITE

BRAND NAME RECIPES

Publications International, Ltd.

Favorite Brand Name Recipes at www.fbnr.com

Microwave Cooking: Microwave ovens vary in wattage. Use the cooking times as guidelines and check for doneness before adding more time.

Preparation/Cooking Times: Preparation times are based on the approximate amount of time required to assemble the recipe before cooking, baking, chilling or serving. These times include preparation steps such as measuring, chopping and mixing. The fact that some preparations and cooking can be done simultaneously is taken into account. Preparation of optional ingredients and serving suggestions is not included.

100 BEST FAVORITE BRAND NAME RECIPES

All-American Favorites from the Brands You Trust

Good recipes are like good friends—you can always depend on them. Chances are you already have a recipe box filled with well-used, food-stained index cards. If some of your favorites came from the back of a box or the label on a jar, then this cookbook is for you.

You'll find the very best recipes developed over the years in test kitchens across the country. Some may be familiar, like classic green bean casserole or California dip. Others will be a delightful surprise. Every recipe has been tested extensively by home economists at the food companies whose brands are featured. You can be sure these recipes will not only work, they'll wow you every time. After all, who knows better how to get the best out of their products than the companies who make them?

Because this book was written with the home cook in mind, dishes are designed for families, not fancy restaurants. (Although some of the fabulous desserts included here would put many restaurants to shame!) There are no hard-to-find exotic ingredients in these recipes, no expensive equipment to buy, no tricky techniques to master. In fact, you can pull together many of the dishes from ingredients already in your pantry.

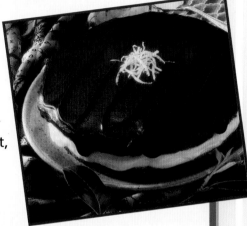

From cookies to casseroles, fajitas to lasagna, this book is a celebration of America's unique way with food. No place else on earth offers such a diverse array of flavors and choices. Indulge your family's taste for Mexican food with a taco salad recipe from Ortega®. Take Miracle Whip®'s Great American Potato Salad on a picnic or impress the gang with Hershey's Classic Boston Cream Pie.

Whether you're searching for a fancy dessert to take to the bake sale or a quick treat for Sunday night supper for the family, you'll find the best ideas right here in *100 Best Favorite Brand Name Recipes.*

Classic Chicken Puffs

- **1 box UNCLE BEN'S® Long Grain & Wild Rice Original Recipe**
- **2 cups cubed cooked TYSON® Fresh Chicken**
- **½ can (10¾ ounces) condensed cream of mushroom soup**
- **⅓ cup chopped green onions**
- **⅓ cup diced pimientos or diced red bell pepper**
- **⅓ cup diced celery**
- **⅓ cup chopped fresh parsley**
- **⅓ cup chopped slivered almonds**
- **¼ cup milk**
- **1 box frozen prepared puff pastry shells, thawed**

COOK: CLEAN: Wash hands. Prepare rice according to package directions. When rice is done, add remaining ingredients (except pastry shells). Mix well. Reheat 1 minute. Fill pastry shells with rice mixture.

SERVE: Serve with a mixed green salad and balsamic vinaigrette, if desired.

CHILL: Refrigerate leftovers immediately.

Makes 6 servings

Note: This recipe is a great way to use up leftover chicken.

Prep Time: none
Cook Time: 20 minutes

Classic Chicken Puff

Cheesy Quesadillas

½ **pound ground beef**
1 **medium onion, chopped**
¼ **teaspoon salt**
1 **can (4½ ounces) chopped green chilies, drained**
1 **jar (26 to 28 ounces) RAGÚ® Robusto!™ Pasta Sauce**
8 **(6½-inch) flour tortillas**
1 **tablespoon olive or vegetable oil**
2 **cups shredded Cheddar and/or mozzarella cheese (about**
   8 ounces)

1. Preheat oven to 400°F. In 12-inch skillet, brown ground beef with onion and salt over medium-high heat; drain. Stir in chilies and ½ cup Ragú Pasta Sauce; set aside.

2. Meanwhile, evenly brush one side of 4 tortillas with half of the oil. On cookie sheets, arrange tortillas, oil-side down. Evenly top with ½ of the cheese, beef filling, then remaining cheese. Top with remaining 4 tortillas, then brush tops with remaining oil.

3. Bake 10 minutes or until cheese is melted. To serve, cut each quesadilla into 4 wedges. Serve with remaining sauce, heated.

Makes 4 servings

Prep Time: 10 minutes
Cook Time: 15 minutes

Cheesy Quesadilla

The Famous Lipton® California Dip

1 envelope LIPTON® RECIPE SECRETS® Onion Soup Mix
1 container (16 ounces) regular or light sour cream

1. In medium bowl, blend all ingredients; chill at least 2 hours.

2. Serve with your favorite dippers.   *Makes about 2 cups dip*

Note: For a creamier dip, add more sour cream.

Sensational Spinach Dip: Add 1 package (10 ounces) frozen chopped spinach, thawed and squeezed dry.

California Seafood Dip: Add 1 cup finely chopped cooked clams, crabmeat or shrimp, ¼ cup chili sauce and 1 tablespoon horseradish.

California Bacon Dip: Add ⅓ cup crumbled cooked bacon or bacon bits.

California Blue Cheese Dip: Add ¼ pound crumbled blue cheese and ¼ cup finely chopped walnuts.

BEST DIP TIP
Chips are great, but dips also work well with veggies, like baby carrots, cherry tomatoes and pepper strips. Try breadsticks, pita triangles or bagel chips for a change of pace, too.

Bandito Buffalo Wings

1 package (1¼ ounces) ORTEGA® Taco Seasoning Mix
12 (about 1 pound *total*) chicken wings
ORTEGA® SALSA (any flavor)

PREHEAT oven to 375°F. Lightly grease 13×9-inch baking pan.

PLACE seasoning mix in heavy-duty plastic or paper bag. Add 3 chicken wings; shake well to coat. Place wings in prepared pan. Repeat until all wings have been coated.

BAKE for 35 to 40 minutes or until no longer pink near bone. Serve with salsa for dipping.   *Makes 6 appetizer servings*

SPAM™ Pinwheels

1 (1-pound) loaf frozen bread dough, thawed
¼ cup pizza sauce
1 (7-ounce) can SPAM® Classic, cubed
2 cups (8 ounces) shredded mozzarella cheese
2 tablespoons chopped pepperoncini
Additional pizza sauce

Roll bread dough out onto lightly floured surface to 12-inch square. Brush pizza sauce over bread dough. Sprinkle SPAM®, cheese and pepperoncini over dough. Roll dough, jelly-roll fashion; pinch seam to seal (do not seal ends). Cut roll into 16 slices. Place slices, cut side down, on greased baking sheet. Cover and let rise in warm place 45 minutes. Heat oven to 350°F. Bake 20 to 25 minutes or until golden brown. Serve immediately with additional pizza sauce.

Makes 16 appetizer servings

Baked Cream Cheese Appetizer

1 can (4 ounces) refrigerated crescent dinner rolls
1 package (8 ounces) PHILADELPHIA® Cream Cheese
½ teaspoon dill weed
1 egg white, beaten

UNROLL dough on lightly greased cookie sheet; firmly press perforations together to form 12×4-inch rectangle.

SPRINKLE cream cheese with dill; lightly press dill into cream cheese. Place cream cheese, dill-side up, in center of dough. Bring edges of dough up over cream cheese; press edges of dough together to seal, completely enclosing cream cheese. Brush with egg white.

BAKE at 350°F for 15 to 18 minutes or until lightly browned. Serve with NABISCO® Crackers, French bread or fresh fruit slices.

Makes 8 servings

Substitutes: Substitute ½ teaspoon dried rosemary leaves, crushed, combined with ½ teaspoon paprika for the dill weed.

Prep Time: 10 minutes
Bake Time: 18 minutes

Hot Artichoke and Tuna Spread

1 (3-ounce) pouch of STARKIST® Premium Albacore or Chunk Light
    Tuna
1 jar (12 ounces) marinated artichoke hearts, drained
1 cup shredded mozzarella cheese
½ cup grated Parmesan cheese
¼ cup chopped canned green chilies
1 to 2 cloves garlic
2 to 3 tablespoons mayonnaise
1 tablespoon minced green onion
    Hot pepper sauce to taste
    French bread or assorted crackers

In food processor bowl with metal blade, place all ingredients except
bread. Process until well blended but not puréed. Transfer mixture to
ovenproof serving dish. Bake, uncovered, in 350°F oven about
30 minutes or until mixture is golden. Serve hot with French bread.

Makes 12 servings

Variation: This mixture may be baked in small hollowed bread shell.
Wrap in foil; bake as above. Open top of foil last 5 minutes of baking.

Note: Mixture keeps well, tightly covered, in refrigerator for up to
5 days.

Prep Time: 35 minutes

Devilish Eggs

12 hard-cooked eggs, cut in half
 6 tablespoons low-fat mayonnaise
 2 tablespoons *French's*® Classic Yellow® Mustard
 ¼ teaspoon salt
 ⅛ teaspoon ground red pepper

1. Remove yolk from egg whites using teaspoon. Press yolks through sieve with back of spoon or mash with fork in medium bowl. Stir in mayonnaise, mustard, salt and pepper; mix well.

2. Spoon or pipe yolk mixture into egg whites. Arrange on serving platter. Garnish as desired. Cover; chill in refrigerator until ready to serve.   *Makes 12 servings*

Variations: Stir in one of the following: 2 tablespoons minced red onion plus 1 tablespoon horseradish, 2 tablespoons pickle relish plus 1 tablespoon minced fresh dill, 2 tablespoons each minced onion and celery plus 1 tablespoon minced fresh dill, ¼ cup (1 ounce) shredded Cheddar cheese plus ½ teaspoon *French's*® Worcestershire Sauce.

Prep Time: 40 minutes
Chill Time: 30 minutes

BEST WAY TO HARD COOK EGGS
Place eggs in a single layer in a saucepan. Add cold water to cover eggs by an inch. Cover and bring water to a boil. Remove from heat and let stand, covered, 15 minutes. Immediately pour off water, cover with cold water or ice water and let stand until cooled completely.

Devilish Eggs

Chili Chip Party Platter

    1 pound ground beef
    1 medium onion, chopped
    1 package (1.48 ounces) LAWRY'S® Spices & Seasonings for Chili
    1 can (6 ounces) tomato paste
    1 cup water
    1 bag (8 to 9 ounces) tortilla chips or corn chips
1½ cups (6 ounces) shredded cheddar cheese
    1 can (2¼ ounces) sliced pitted black olives, drained
 ½ cup sliced green onions

In medium skillet, cook ground beef until browned and crumbly; drain fat. Add onion, Spices & Seasonings for Chili, tomato paste and water; mix well. Bring to a boil over medium-high heat; reduce heat to low and simmer, uncovered, 15 minutes, stirring occasionally. Serve over tortilla chips. Top with cheddar cheese, olives and green onions.

Makes 4 servings

Serving Suggestion: Serve with a cool beverage and sliced melon.

Ortega® Green Chile Guacamole

    2 medium very ripe avocados, seeded, peeled and mashed
    1 can (4 ounces) ORTEGA® Diced Green Chiles
    2 large green onions, chopped
    2 tablespoons olive oil
    1 teaspoon lime juice
    1 clove garlic, finely chopped
 ¼ teaspoon salt
    Tortilla chips

COMBINE avocados, chiles, green onions, olive oil, lime juice, garlic and salt in medium bowl. Cover; refrigerate for at least 1 hour. Serve with chips.

Makes 2 cups

Serving Suggestions: This all-time favorite dip can be used in tacos, burritos, tamales, chimichangas or combined with ORTEGA® SALSA for a spicy salad dressing.

East Meets West Cocktail Franks

1 cup prepared sweet and sour sauce
1½ tablespoons rice vinegar or cider vinegar
1 tablespoon grated fresh ginger *or* **1 teaspoon dried ginger**
1 tablespoon dark sesame oil
½ teaspoon chile oil (optional)
1 package (12 ounces) HEBREW NATIONAL® Cocktail Beef Franks
2 tablespoons chopped cilantro or chives

Combine sweet and sour sauce, vinegar, ginger, sesame oil and chile oil in medium saucepan. Bring to a boil over medium heat. Cook 5 minutes or until thickened. Add cocktail franks; cover and cook until heated through. Transfer to chafing dish; sprinkle with cilantro. Serve with frilled wooden picks.

Makes 12 appetizer servings (2 cocktail franks per serving)

Velveeta® Con Queso Dip

1 pound (16 ounces) VELVEETA® Pasteurized Prepared Cheese
    Product, cut up
1 can (10 ounces) diced tomatoes and green chilies, drained

1. Microwave VELVEETA and tomatoes and green chilies in 1½-quart microwavable bowl on HIGH 5 minutes or until VELVEETA is melted, stirring after 3 minutes. Serve hot with tortilla chips.

Makes 2¼ cups

Prep Time: 5 minutes
Microwave Time: 5 minutes

East Meets West Cocktail Franks

Savory Seafood Spread

2 packages (8 ounces each) light cream cheese, softened
1 package (8 ounces) imitation crab meat, flaked
2 tablespoons minced green onion
1 tablespoon prepared horseradish
1 tablespoon *Frank's® RedHot®* Cayenne Pepper Sauce
1 teaspoon *French's®* Worcestershire Sauce
½ cup sliced almonds
  Paprika
  Crackers
  Vegetable dippers

1. Preheat oven to 375°F. Beat or process cream cheese in electric mixer or food processor until smooth and creamy. Add crab, onion, horseradish, *Frank's RedHot* Sauce and Worcestershire; beat or process until well blended.

2. Spread cream cheese mixture onto 9-inch pie plate. Top with almonds and sprinkle with paprika. Bake 20 minutes or until mixture is heated through and almonds are golden.

3. Serve with crackers or vegetable dippers.   *Makes 3 cups spread*

Prep Time: 10 minutes
Cook Time: 20 minutes

Mini Crab Cakes

1 pound crabmeat
1 cup fine, dry bread crumbs, divided
2 eggs, beaten
¼ cup minced onion
¼ cup minced green bell pepper
¼ cup minced red bell pepper
1 teaspoon dry mustard
½ teaspoon TABASCO® brand Pepper Sauce
Salt to taste
Vegetable oil
Zesty Remoulade Sauce (recipe follows)

Combine crabmeat, ½ cup bread crumbs, eggs, onion, bell peppers, mustard, TABASCO® Sauce and salt in large bowl. Cover and refrigerate 1 to 2 hours or until mixture becomes firm. Shape mixture into small cakes, about 1½×1 inches. Coat cakes in remaining ½ cup bread crumbs.

Pour oil into heavy skillet to depth of ⅓ inch; heat skillet over medium heat. When oil is hot, cook crab cakes about 3 to 5 minutes on each side or until browned. Remove to paper towels. Serve crab cakes warm; top with dollops of Zesty Remoulade Sauce.

Makes 20 to 25 cakes

Zesty Remoulade Sauce

1 cup mayonnaise
2 to 3 green onions, finely chopped
1 rib celery, finely chopped
2 tablespoons prepared horseradish, drained
1 tablespoon finely chopped chives
1 tablespoon Dijon mustard
1 tablespoon fresh lemon juice
1 clove garlic, finely chopped
½ teaspoon TABASCO® brand Pepper Sauce

Combine all ingredients in medium bowl. Cover and refrigerate 1 hour to blend flavors. Serve chilled.

Makes 1¾ cups

Mini Crab Cakes with Zesty Remoulade Sauce

Barbecued Swedish Meatballs

MEATBALLS
1½ pounds lean ground beef
1 cup finely chopped onions
½ cup fresh breadcrumbs
½ cup HOLLAND HOUSE® White Cooking Wine
1 egg, beaten
½ teaspoon allspice
½ teaspoon nutmeg

SAUCE
1 jar (10 ounces) currant jelly
½ cup chili sauce
¼ cup HOLLAND HOUSE® White Cooking Wine
1 tablespoon cornstarch

Heat oven to 350°F. In medium bowl, combine all meatball ingredients; mix well. Shape into 1-inch balls. Place meatballs in 15×10×1-inch baking pan. Bake 20 minutes or until brown.

In medium saucepan, combine all sauce ingredients; mix well. Cook over medium heat until mixture boils and thickens, stirring occasionally. Add meatballs. To serve, place meatballs and sauce in fondue pot or chafing dish. Serve with cocktail picks.

Makes 6 to 8 servings

BEST WAY TO SHAPE MEATBALLS
Place meat mixture on a cutting board and pat evenly into a large square, one inch thick. Divide meat into one-inch squares with a knife, then pick up each square and shape it into a ball.

Honey Popcorn Clusters

   Vegetable cooking spray
 6 cups air-popped popcorn
⅔ cup DOLE® Golden or Seedless Raisins
½ cup DOLE® Chopped Dates or Pitted Dates, chopped
⅓ cup almonds (optional)
⅓ cup packed brown sugar
¼ cup honey
 2 tablespoons margarine
¼ teaspoon baking soda

• Line bottom and sides of 13×9-inch baking pan with large sheet of aluminum foil. Spray foil with vegetable cooking spray.

• Stir together popcorn, raisins, dates and almonds in foil-lined pan.

• Combine brown sugar, honey and margarine in small saucepan. Bring to boil over medium heat, stirring constantly; reduce heat to low. Cook 5 minutes. *Do not stir.* Remove from heat.

• Stir in baking soda. Pour evenly over popcorn mixture, stirring quickly to coat mixture evenly.

• Bake at 300°F 12 to 15 minutes or until mixture is lightly browned, stirring once halfway through baking time.

• Lift foil from pan; place on cooling rack. Cool popcorn mixture completely; break into clusters. Popcorn can be stored in airtight container up to 1 week.   *Makes 7 cups*

Prep Time: 20 minutes
Bake Time: 15 minutes

Tuna Noodle Casserole

1 can (10¾ ounces) condensed cream of mushroom soup
1 cup milk
3 cups hot cooked rotini pasta (2 cups uncooked)
1 can (12 ounces) tuna packed in water, drained and
    flaked
1⅓ cups *French's*® French Fried Onions, divided
1 package (10 ounces) frozen peas and carrots
½ cup (2 ounces) shredded Cheddar or grated Parmesan
    cheese

MICROWAVE DIRECTIONS
Combine soup and milk in 2-quart microwavable shallow casserole. Stir in pasta, tuna, ⅔ *cup* French Fried Onions, vegetables and cheese. Cover; microwave on HIGH 10 minutes* or until heated through, stirring halfway through cooking time. Top with remaining ⅔ *cup* onions. Microwave 1 minute or until onions are golden.

Makes 6 servings

Or, bake, covered, in 350°F oven 25 to 30 minutes.

Tip: Garnish with chopped pimiento and parsley sprigs, if desired.

Prep Time: 10 minutes
Cook Time: 11 minutes

32

Fajitas

½ **cup chopped onion**
¼ **cup GRANDMA'S® Molasses**
¼ **cup oil**
2 **tablespoons ROSE'S® Lime Juice**
2 **tablespoons chili powder**
½ **teaspoon oregano leaves**
2 **cloves garlic, minced**
1 **pound boneless top round or sirloin steak, cut into thin strips**
10 **flour tortillas (8 to 10 inches), warmed**
½ **cup (2 ounces) shredded Monterey Jack cheese**
2 **cups refried beans**
2 **tomatoes, chopped**
1½ **cups shredded lettuce**
1 **avocado, chopped**
1 **cup salsa**
Sour cream

1. In medium plastic bowl, combine onion, molasses, oil, lime juice, chili powder, oregano and garlic. Mix well. Add steak, stir to coat. Cover; marinate 4 to 6 hours or overnight, stirring occasionally.

2. In large skillet, stir-fry meat mixture 5 minutes or until brown. To serve, place meat in center of each tortilla; top with cheese, refried beans, tomatoes, lettuce, avocado and salsa. Fold up tortilla. Serve with sour cream. *Makes 5 servings*

FAVORITE WAY TO SERVE FAJITAS
Serve warmed tortillas wrapped in a clean kitchen towel in a basket. Offer the meat and other fixings in separate serving dishes. Everyone can have fun helping themselves and creating fajitas with their favorite ingredients.

Classic Family Lasagna

1 package (1 pound) TYSON® Fresh Ground Chicken
1 medium onion, chopped
½ cup chopped green bell pepper (optional)
2 cloves garlic, minced
1 jar (30 ounces) spaghetti sauce
1 container (15 ounces) ricotta cheese
¾ cup grated Parmesan cheese, divided
1 egg, beaten
¼ teaspoon black pepper
9 lasagna noodles, cooked according to package directions
3½ cups (14 ounces) shredded mozzarella cheese

PREP: Preheat oven to 375°F. CLEAN: Wash hands. In large skillet, cook and stir chicken, onion, bell pepper and garlic over medium-high heat until chicken is no longer pink. Stir in sauce; heat through and set aside. In medium bowl, combine ricotta cheese, ½ cup Parmesan cheese, egg and black pepper; mix well. Spray 13×9-inch baking dish with nonstick cooking spray. Spread ⅓ cup sauce on bottom of dish. Top with 3 noodles, one third of sauce, one third of ricotta mixture and 1 cup mozzarella cheese. Repeat layers twice, except do not top with remaining 1½ cups mozzarella cheese. Cover tightly with foil sprayed lightly with nonstick cooking spray.

COOK: Bake 40 minutes. Remove foil. Top with remaining cheese. Bake 15 minutes or until bubbly and cheese is melted.

SERVE: Serve with a green salad and garlic bread, if desired.

CHILL: Refrigerate leftovers immediately.   *Makes 12 servings*

Prep Time: 35 minutes
Cook Time: 1 hour

Big D Ranch Burgers

1 cup sliced onions
⅓ cup green bell pepper strips
⅓ cup red bell pepper strips
1 tablespoon margarine or butter
3 tablespoons A.1.® Steak Sauce
2 teaspoons prepared horseradish
1 pound ground beef
4 onion rolls, split

Cook onions, green pepper and red pepper in margarine or butter in skillet over medium heat until tender-crisp. Stir in steak sauce and horseradish; keep warm.

Shape ground beef into 4 burgers. Grill burgers over medium heat for 5 minutes on each side or until desired doneness. Place burgers on roll bottoms; top each with ¼ cup pepper mixture and roll top. Serve immediately.   *Makes 4 servings*

BEST WAY TO SEED AND SLICE PEPPERS
First remove the stem by cutting around the top with a paring knife. Pull out the stem and most of the seeds will come with it. Slice off the bottom of the pepper, then divide the pepper into two or three sections. Lay the sections flat, remove remaining seeds and ribs, then slice into strips.

Spaghetti with Meat and Mushroom Sauce

1 package (16 ounces) BARILLA® Spaghetti or Thick Spaghetti
1 large onion, chopped
2 tablespoons minced garlic
¼ cup olive oil
1 pound loin strip steak, cut into ½-inch cubes
2½ cups (6 ounces) sliced mushrooms
1 cup chopped red, yellow and green bell peppers
1 medium tomato, chopped
1 jar (26 ounces) BARILLA® Tomato and Basil Pasta Sauce
¼ cup red wine
1 tablespoon dried Italian seasoning
Salt and pepper
Grated Parmesan cheese

1. Cook spaghetti according to package directions; drain.

2. Meanwhile, cook onion and garlic in olive oil in Dutch oven or large pot over medium heat until onion is transparent. Add steak; cook and stir over medium-high heat 4 minutes. Add vegetables; cook and stir 4 minutes. Stir in pasta sauce, wine and Italian seasoning; heat just to boiling, stirring frequently. Add salt and pepper to taste.

3. Combine sauce with hot drained spaghetti. Cover and let stand 2 minutes before serving. Serve with cheese.

Makes 8 to 10 servings

Tip: To enhance flavor, substitute ¼ cup finely chopped fresh herbs for 1 tablespoon dried Italian seasoning.

Chicken Walnut Stir-Fry

SAUCE
- ⅔ cup chicken broth
- 1½ tablespoons LA CHOY® Soy Sauce
- 1 tablespoon cornstarch
- 1 tablespoon dry sherry
- ½ teaspoon sugar
- ¼ teaspoon pepper
- ¼ teaspoon Asian sesame oil

CHICKEN AND VEGETABLES
- 2 tablespoons cornstarch
- 2 teaspoons LA CHOY® Soy Sauce
- 2 teaspoons dry sherry
- 1 pound boneless skinless chicken breasts, cut into thin 2-inch strips
- 4 tablespoons WESSON® Oil, divided
- 2½ cups fresh broccoli florets
- 1½ teaspoons minced fresh garlic
- 1 teaspoon minced ginger root
- 1 can (8 ounces) LA CHOY® Bamboo Shoots, drained
- 1 cup toasted chopped walnuts
- 1 package (6 ounces) frozen pea pods, thawed and drained
- 1 can (5 ounces) LA CHOY® Chow Mein Noodles, optional

In small bowl, combine sauce ingredients; set aside. In separate small bowl, combine 2 tablespoons cornstarch, soy sauce and sherry; mix well. Add chicken; toss gently to coat. In large nonstick skillet or wok, heat 3 tablespoons Wesson Oil. Add half of chicken mixture; stir-fry until chicken is no longer pink in center. Remove chicken from skillet; set aside. Repeat with remaining chicken mixture. Heat remaining 1 tablespoon Wesson Oil in same skillet. Add broccoli, garlic and ginger; stir-fry until broccoli is crisp-tender. Return chicken mixture to skillet with bamboo shoots, walnuts and pea pods; heat thoroughly, stirring occasionally. Stir sauce; add to skillet. Cook, stirring constantly, until sauce is thick and bubbly. Garnish with La Choy Chow Mein Noodles, if desired. *Makes 4 to 6 servings*

Cheese-Stuffed Meat Loaf

1½ pounds ground beef
1 jar (26 to 28 ounces) RAGÚ® Chunky Gardenstyle Pasta Sauce
1 large egg, slightly beaten
¼ cup plain dry bread crumbs
2 cups shredded mozzarella cheese (about 8 ounces)
1 tablespoon finely chopped fresh parsley

1. Preheat oven to 350°F. In large bowl, combine ground beef, ⅓ cup Ragú Pasta Sauce, egg and bread crumbs. Season, if desired, with salt and ground black pepper. In 13×9-inch baking or roasting pan, shape into 12×8-inch rectangle.

2. Sprinkle 1½ cups cheese and parsley down center leaving ¾-inch border. Roll, starting at long end, jelly-roll style. Press ends together to seal.

3. Bake uncovered 45 minutes. Pour remaining sauce over meat loaf and sprinkle with remaining ½ cup cheese. Bake an additional 15 minutes or until sauce is heated through and cheese is melted. Let stand 5 minutes before serving.   *Makes 6 servings*

Tip: Molding the meat mixture onto waxed paper helps make rolling easier. Just lift waxed paper to curl the meat over cheese filling, then carefully remove meat from paper. Continue rolling in this manner until filling is enclosed in roll and meat is off paper.

Prep Time: 20 minutes
Cook Time: 1 hour

Baked Ham with Apple-Raspberry Sauce

   1 (3-pound) canned ham
   1 cup chopped apples
  ½ cup SMUCKER'S® Red Raspberry Preserves
  ½ cup SMUCKER'S® Apple Jelly
  ¾ cup apple cider
   1 tablespoon cider vinegar
   2 tablespoons cornstarch
     Endive or parsley sprigs
     Whole crabapples

Bake ham according to package directions.

Mix chopped apples, preserves and jelly in medium saucepan. Combine cider, vinegar and cornstarch; stir into saucepan. Heat to boiling; boil, stirring constantly, until thickened, about 1 minute.

Slice ham and arrange on platter; garnish with endive and crabapples. Serve with sauce. *Makes 8 to 10 servings*

Cowboy Franks & Beans

   1 jar (26 to 28 ounces) RAGÚ® Old World Style® Pasta Sauce
   1 can (19 ounces) red kidney beans, rinsed and drained
   4 frankfurters, cut into ¼-inch pieces
   8 ounces wagon wheel pasta, cooked and drained
  ½ cup shredded mozzarella or Cheddar cheese (about 2 ounces)

1. In 3-quart saucepan, cook Ragú Pasta Sauce, beans and frankfurters over medium heat, stirring occasionally, 10 minutes or until heated through.

2. To serve, toss pasta with sauce mixture and sprinkle with cheese.
Makes 4 servings

Prep Time: 5 minutes
Cook Time: 10 minutes

Parmesan Fried Chicken

1 egg
2 tablespoons water
⅔ cup fine, dry bread crumbs
⅓ cup grated Parmesan cheese
2 teaspoons LAWRY'S® Lemon Pepper
1 teaspoon LAWRY'S® Seasoned Salt
2½ to 3 pounds chicken pieces
¼ cup butter
2 tablespoons salad oil

In shallow dish, beat egg and water. In large plastic resealable food storage bag, combine bread crumbs, cheese, Lemon Pepper and Seasoned Salt; mix well. Dip chicken pieces in egg, then shake in bag with bread crumbs. In large skillet, heat butter and oil together. Add chicken pieces, a few at a time and cook over medium-high heat, removing pieces as they brown. When all are browned, return all chicken to skillet, cover and cook over low heat 25 to 30 minutes or until tender and juices run clear. Remove cover during last 5 minutes to crisp.   *Makes 4 to 6 servings*

Serving Suggestion: Serve with tossed green salad and Johannisberg Riesling or Gamay Beaujolais.

Country Sausage Macaroni and Cheese

1 pound BOB EVANS® Special Seasonings Roll Sausage
1½ cups milk
12 ounces pasteurized processed Cheddar cheese, cut into cubes
½ cup Dijon mustard
1 cup diced fresh or drained canned tomatoes
1 cup sliced mushrooms
⅓ cup sliced green onions
⅛ teaspoon cayenne pepper
12 ounces uncooked elbow macaroni
2 tablespoons grated Parmesan cheese

Preheat oven to 350°F. Crumble and cook sausage in medium skillet until browned. Drain on paper towels. Combine milk, processed cheese and mustard in medium saucepan; cook and stir over low heat until cheese melts and mixture is smooth. Stir in sausage, tomatoes, mushrooms, green onions and cayenne pepper. Remove from heat.

Cook macaroni according to package directions; drain. Combine hot macaroni and cheese mixture in large bowl; toss until well coated. Spoon into greased shallow 2-quart casserole dish. Cover and bake 15 to 20 minutes. Stir; sprinkle with Parmesan cheese. Bake, uncovered, 5 minutes more. Let stand 10 minutes before serving. Refrigerate leftovers.   *Makes 6 to 8 servings*

Marinated Pork Roast

½ **cup GRANDMA'S® Molasses**
½ **cup Dijon mustard**
¼ **cup tarragon vinegar**
   Boneless pork loin roast (3 to 4 pounds)

1. In large plastic bowl, combine molasses, mustard and tarragon vinegar; mix well. Add pork to molasses mixture, turning to coat all sides. Marinate 1 to 2 hours at room temperature or overnight covered in refrigerator, turning several times.

2. Heat oven to 325°F. Remove pork from marinade; reserve marinade. Place pork in shallow roasting pan. Cook for 1 to 2 hours or until meat thermometer inserted into thickest part of roast reaches 160°F, basting with marinade* every 30 minutes; discard remaining marinade.

Makes 6 to 8 servings

*Do not baste during last 5 minutes of cooking.

BEST WAY TO MARINATE
Put meat and marinade in a heavy-duty resealable plastic bag and you'll have an easy way to turn the meat occasionally to ensure that it marinates evenly. Squeeze as much air out of the bag as you can before closing so the surface of the meat stays in contact with the marinade.

Marinated Pork Roast with Baked Apple (page 216)

California Chicken Pot Pies

1 (9-inch) folded refrigerated unbaked pie crust
1 can (10¾ ounces) condensed cream of chicken soup
1 cup half 'n' half or milk
2 cups (10 ounces) cooked chicken, cut into ½-inch cubes
1 bag (16 ounces) California-style frozen vegetable combination,
    such as cauliflower, carrots and asparagus, thawed and
    drained*
1⅓ cups *French's*® French Fried Onions, divided
¼ teaspoon dried thyme leaves
½ cup (2 ounces) shredded Swiss cheese

Or, substitute any package of combination vegetables for California-style vegetables.

Preheat oven to 400°F. Roll out pie crust onto lightly floured board. Invert 10-ounce custard cup on top of crust. With sharp knife, trace around cup and cut out circle; prick several times with fork. Repeat 5 more times, rerolling scraps of pie crust as necessary. Cover; set crusts aside.

Combine soup and half 'n' half in large bowl. Stir in chicken, vegetables, ⅔ *cup* French Fried Onions and thyme. Spoon mixture evenly into 6 (10-ounce) custard cups. Place filled cups on baking sheet. Place 1 crust over each cup. Bake, uncovered, 30 minutes or until crust is browned.

Sprinkle crusts with cheese; top with remaining ⅔ *cup* onions. Bake 1 minute or until onions are golden.   *Makes 6 servings*

Note: Filling may be baked in 9-inch pie plate. Top with uncut 9-inch pie crust. Bake at 400°F 35 minutes or until crust is golden. Top with cheese and remaining ⅔ cup onions. Bake 1 minute or until onions are golden.

Prep Time: 15 minutes
Cook Time: 31 minutes

Classic Pepperoni Pizza

1 cup (½ of 15 ounce can) CONTADINA® Original Pizza Sauce
1 (12-inch) prepared, pre-baked pizza crust
1½ cups (6 ounces) shredded mozzarella cheese, divided
1½ ounces sliced pepperoni
1 tablespoon chopped fresh parsley

1. Spread pizza sauce onto crust to within 1 inch of edge.

2. Sprinkle with 1 cup cheese, pepperoni and remaining cheese.

3. Bake according to pizza crust package directions or until crust is crisp and cheese is melted. Sprinkle with parsley.   *Makes 8 servings*

Creamy Chicken Broccoli Skillet

½ cup MIRACLE WHIP® Salad Dressing
1 pound boneless skinless chicken breasts, cubed
1 package (10 ounces) frozen chopped broccoli, thawed *or* 2 cups
     fresh broccoli flowerets
½ pound (8 ounces) VELVEETA® Pasteurized Prepared Cheese
     Product, cut up
2 cups hot cooked MINUTE® White Rice

• HEAT salad dressing in large skillet on medium heat. Add chicken; cook and stir about 8 minutes or until cooked through.

• ADD 2 cups water, broccoli and VELVEETA. Bring to a boil.

• STIR in rice; cover. Remove from heat. Let stand 5 minutes.
Makes 4 servings

Prep Time: 10 minutes
Cook Time: 15 minutes plus standing

Country Chicken Stew

2 tablespoons butter or margarine
1 pound boneless skinless chicken breasts, cut into 1-inch cubes
½ pound small red potatoes, cut into ½-inch cubes
2 tablespoons cooking sherry
2 jars (12 ounces each) golden chicken gravy
1 bag (16 ounces) BIRDS EYE® frozen Farm Fresh Mixtures Broccoli,
    Green Beans, Pearl Onions and Red Peppers
½ cup water

• Melt butter in large saucepan over high heat. Add chicken and potatoes; cook about 8 minutes or until browned, stirring frequently.

• Add sherry; cook until evaporated. Add gravy, vegetables and water.

• Bring to boil; reduce heat to medium-low. Cover and cook 6 to 7 minutes.   *Makes 4 to 6 servings*

Prep Time: 5 minutes
Cook Time: 20 minutes

BEST WAY TO HANDLE CHICKEN SAFELY
Thoroughly wash cutting surfaces, utensils and your hands with hot soapy water after preparing raw chicken. This eliminates the risk of contaminating other foods (especially those that won't be cooked) with the salmonella bacteria that is often present in raw chicken.

Roast Beef with Red Wine Gravy

2 tablespoons oil
1 sirloin tip roast (3 to 4 pounds)
   Salt and black pepper
2 tablespoons all-purpose flour
1 jar (7 ounces) cocktail onions, drained
1 can (14½ ounces) beef broth
2 tablespoons HOLLAND HOUSE® Red Cooking Wine
   Sherried Mushrooms (recipe follows)

Heat oven to 350°F. Heat oil in Dutch oven. Season roast to taste with salt and pepper; brown on all sides. Remove from Dutch oven. Drain excess fat, reserving ¼ cup drippings in Dutch oven. Sprinkle flour over reserved drippings. Cook over medium heat until lightly browned, stirring constantly. Add roast and onions to Dutch oven. Roast for 1¾ to 2¼ hours or until desired doneness. Remove roast to cutting board. Let stand 5 to 10 minutes before slicing. Gradually stir in beef broth and cooking wine. Bring to a boil; reduce heat. Cook until gravy thickens. Slice roast and arrange with onions on serving platter. Serve with gravy and Sherried Mushrooms.

Makes 6 servings

Sherried Mushrooms

½ cup butter
1 cup HOLLAND HOUSE® Sherry Cooking Wine
1 clove garlic, crushed
18 fresh mushrooms, sliced
   Salt and black pepper

Melt butter in medium skillet over medium heat. Add cooking wine and garlic. Add mushrooms; cook until tender, about 5 minutes, stirring frequently. Season to taste with salt and pepper.

Makes 2 to 3 servings

QUICK & EASY CLASSICS

Shrimp Creole Pronto

2 tablespoons oil
1 cup chopped onions
1 cup chopped celery
1 green bell pepper, chopped
2 cloves garlic, minced
2 cups chopped peeled tomatoes
1 pound fresh or frozen and thawed uncooked shrimp, peeled, deveined
1 can (8 ounces) tomato sauce
½ cup HOLLAND HOUSE® Marsala Cooking Wine
¼ teaspoon freshly ground black pepper
¼ to ½ teaspoon hot pepper sauce
4 cups hot cooked rice *or* 1 (10-ounce) package of egg noodles, cooked, drained

Heat oil in large saucepan over medium-high heat. Add onions, celery, bell pepper and garlic; cook 2 to 3 minutes. Add tomatoes; cook 2 to 3 minutes, stirring occasionally. Add remaining ingredients except rice; cook 2 to 3 minutes or until shrimp turn pink. Serve over hot cooked rice.

Makes 4 servings

60

Hearty One-Pot Chicken Stew

12 TYSON® Individually Fresh Frozen® Boneless, Skinless Chicken Tenderloins
1 box UNCLE BEN'S CHEF'S RECIPE™ Traditional Red Beans & Rice
1 can (14½ ounces) diced tomatoes, undrained
3 new red potatoes, unpeeled, cut into 1-inch pieces
2 carrots, sliced ½ inch thick
1 onion, cut into 1-inch pieces

PREP: CLEAN: Wash hands. Remove protective ice glaze from frozen chicken by holding under cool running water 1 to 2 minutes. Cut into 1-inch pieces. CLEAN: Wash hands.

COOK: In large saucepan, combine chicken, beans and rice, contents of seasoning packet, 2¼ cups water, tomatoes, potatoes, carrots and onion. Bring to a boil. Cover, reduce heat; simmer 20 minutes or until internal juices of chicken run clear. (Or insert instant-read meat thermometer in thickest part of chicken. Temperature should read 170°F.)

SERVE: Serve with hot rolls, if desired.

CHILL: Refrigerate leftovers immediately   *Makes 4 servings*

Prep Time: 10 minutes
Cook Time: 20 to 25 minutes

Velveeta® Cheesy Beef Stroganoff

1 pound ground beef
2 cups water
3 cups (6 ounces) medium egg noodles, uncooked
¾ pound (12 ounces) VELVEETA® Pasteurized Prepared Cheese
   Product, cut up
1 can (10¾ ounces) condensed cream of mushroom soup
¼ teaspoon black pepper

1. Brown meat in large skillet; drain.

2. Stir in water. Bring to boil. Stir in noodles. Reduce heat to medium-low; cover. Simmer 8 minutes or until noodles are tender.

3. Add VELVEETA, soup and pepper; stir until VELVEETA is melted.

Makes 4 to 6 servings

Prep Time: 10 minutes
Cook Time: 15 minutes

BEST TIP ON CHOOSING GROUND BEEF

To meet USDA standards, all ground beef must be at least 70 percent lean. Ground sirloin and ground round are the leanest. Ground chuck contains more fat than sirloin or round. It makes juicier hamburgers, but also produces more fat to drain off when browned in a skillet.

Quick 'n' Tangy Beef Stir-Fry

SAUCE
- ½ cup *French's®* Worcestershire Sauce
- ½ cup water
- 2 tablespoons sugar
- 2 teaspoons cornstarch
- ½ teaspoon ground ginger
- ½ teaspoon garlic powder

STIR-FRY
- 1 pound thinly sliced beef steak
- 3 cups sliced bell peppers

1. Combine ingredients for sauce. Marinate beef in ¼ *cup* sauce 5 minutes. Heat *1 tablespoon oil* in large skillet or wok over high heat. Stir-fry beef in batches 5 minutes or until browned.

2. Add peppers; cook 2 minutes. Add remaining sauce; stir-fry until sauce thickens. Serve over hot cooked rice or ramen noodles, if desired.   *Makes 4 servings*

Prep Time: 10 minutes
Cook Time: about 10 minutes

Tuscan Chicken and Pasta

8 ounces BARILLA® Rotini
¼ cup chopped dry-pack sun-dried tomatoes
2 medium zucchini, cut into matchstick strips
1 tablespoon olive or vegetable oil
1 jar (26 ounces) BARILLA® Tomato and Basil Pasta Sauce
1 cup (about 5 ounces) cooked chicken strips (purchased ready-to-eat, frozen or homemade)
¼ cup (1 ounce) grated Parmesan cheese

1. Begin cooking rotini according to package directions. Add sun-dried tomatoes to pasta during last 5 minutes of cooking; drain rotini and tomatoes.

2. Meanwhile, combine zucchini and oil in large (6-cup or more) microwave-safe bowl; cover with plastic wrap. Microwave on HIGH 4 minutes, stirring twice.

3. Stir in pasta sauce and chicken. Cover with plastic wrap; microwave on HIGH 4 minutes, stirring twice. Combine sauce mixture, hot drained rotini with sun-dried tomatoes and cheese; toss to coat.

Makes 6 to 8 servings

BEST WAY TO HANDLE PARMESAN

Domestic and imported Parmesan are available in most supermarkets. To freshly grate, rub cheese across the small holes of a box grater. (Pregrated Parmesan is fine, but it's not as flavorful.) Wrap unused portions of cheese tightly in plastic wrap and store in your refrigerator's cheese compartment.

Quick Italian Spinach Pie

1 container (16 ounces) BREAKSTONE'S® or KNUDSEN® 2% Cottage Cheese
1 package (10 ounces) frozen chopped spinach, thawed, well drained
1 cup KRAFT® Shredded Low-Moisture Part-Skim Mozzarella Cheese
4 eggs, beaten
1 jar (7 ounces) roasted red peppers, well drained, chopped
⅓ cup KRAFT® 100% Grated Parmesan Cheese
1 teaspoon dried oregano leaves

MIX all ingredients.

POUR into greased 9-inch pie plate.

BAKE at 350°F for 40 minutes or until center is set.

Makes 8 servings

Variation: Prepare as directed, substituting ½ cup chopped red pepper for roasted red pepper.

Prep Time: 10 minutes
Bake Time: 40 minutes

Quick Italian Spinach Pie

Tomato Onion Pork Chops

1 tablespoon vegetable oil
4 center-cut pork chops (about ½ inch thick), or 4 boneless, skinless
   chicken breast halves
1 medium onion, chopped
1 cup water
1 package KNORR® Recipe Classics™ Tomato with Basil Soup, Dip
   and Recipe Mix
¼ cup brown sugar
1 tablespoon Worcestershire sauce
   Hot cooked noodles or rice

• In large skillet, heat oil over medium-high heat and brown chops.
Remove chops and set aside. Add onion and cook 2 minutes.

• Stir in water, recipe mix, brown sugar and Worcestershire sauce.
Bring to a boil, stirring occasionally. Return chops to skillet. Reduce
heat to low and simmer covered 8 minutes or until tender.

• To serve, arrange chops over noodles and top with sacue.

Makes 4 servings

Prep Time: 20 minutes
Cook Time: 20 minutes

Easy Turkey and Rice

1 bag SUCCESS® Rice
Vegetable cooking spray
1 tablespoon olive oil
½ pound fresh mushrooms, sliced
¾ cup sliced celery
¼ cup chopped green onions
¼ cup chopped red bell pepper
2 cups chopped cooked turkey
1 can (10¾ ounces) condensed cream of chicken soup
½ cup fat-free mayonnaise
½ cup peanuts (optional)

Prepare rice according to package directions.

Preheat oven to 350°F.

Spray 1½-quart casserole with cooking spray; set aside. Heat oil in large skillet over medium heat. Add vegetables; cook and stir until crisp-tender. Add rice and all remaining ingredients except peanuts; mix lightly. Spoon into prepared casserole. Bake until thoroughly heated, about 25 minutes. Sprinkle with peanuts, if desired.

Makes 4 servings

Fast 'n Easy Chili

1½ pounds ground beef
  1 envelope LIPTON® RECIPE SECRETS® Onion Soup Mix*
  1 can (15 to 19 ounces) red kidney or black beans, drained
1½ cups water
  1 can (8 ounces) tomato sauce
  4 teaspoons chili powder

Also terrific with LIPTON® RECIPE SECRETS® Beefy Mushroom, Onion-Mushroom or Beefy Onion Soup Mix.

1. In 12-inch skillet, brown ground beef over medium-high heat; drain.

2. Stir in remaining ingredients. Bring to a boil over high heat. Reduce heat to low and simmer covered, stirring occasionally, 20 minutes. Serve, if desired, over hot cooked rice.   *Makes 6 servings*

First Alarm Chili: Add 5 teaspoons chili powder.

Second Alarm Chili: Add 2 tablespoons chili powder.

Third Alarm Chili: Add chili powder at your own risk.

BEST TIP ON CHILI POWDER
Chili powder varies not only in terms of heat, but also in terms of ingredients. While they all start with dried, powdered chili peppers, most chili powders also include oregano, cumin, dried garlic and sometimes coriander and cloves, too. Choose one with the combination of flavors and heat you prefer.

Beefy Bean Skillet

1 box (9 ounces) BIRDS EYE® frozen Cut Green Beans
½ pound lean ground beef
½ cup chopped onion
1 cup instant rice
1 can (10 ounces) au jus gravy*
¾ cup ketchup

Or, substitute 1 can (10 ounces) beef broth.

• In medium saucepan, cook green beans according to package directions; drain and set aside.

• Meanwhile, in large skillet, brown beef; drain excess fat. Add onion; cook and stir until onion is tender.

• Add rice, gravy and ketchup. Bring to boil over medium-high heat; cover and reduce heat to medium-low. Simmer 5 to 10 minutes or until rice is cooked, stirring occasionally.

• Stir in beans. Simmer until heated through.   *Makes 4 servings*

Prep Time: 10 minutes
Cook Time: 20 minutes

Beefy Bean Skillet

Quick Mediterranean Fish

1 medium onion, sliced
2 tablespoons olive oil
1 clove garlic, crushed
1 can (14½ ounces) DEL MONTE® Italian Recipe Stewed Tomatoes
3 to 4 tablespoons medium salsa
¼ teaspoon ground cinnamon
1½ pounds firm fish (such as halibut, red snapper or sea bass)
12 stuffed green olives, halved crosswise

MICROWAVE DIRECTIONS

1. Combine onion, oil and garlic in 1½-quart microwavable dish. Cover and microwave on HIGH 3 minutes; drain.

2. Stir in tomatoes, salsa and cinnamon. Top with fish and olives.

3. Cover and microwave on HIGH 3 to 4 minutes or until fish flakes easily with fork. Garnish with chopped parsley, if desired.

Makes 4 to 6 servings

Prep Time: 7 minutes
Microwave Cook Time: 7 minutes

Zesty Lemon-Glazed Steak

½ cup A.1.® Original or A.1.® BOLD & SPICY Steak Sauce
2 teaspoons grated lemon peel
1 clove garlic, minced
¼ teaspoon coarsely ground black pepper
¼ teaspoon dried oregano leaves
4 (4- to 6-ounce) beef shell steaks, about ½-inch thick

Blend steak sauce, lemon peel, garlic, pepper and oregano; brush on both sides of steaks. Grill steaks over medium heat or broil 6 inches from heat source 5 minutes on each side or to desired doneness, basting with sauce occasionally. Serve immediately.

Makes 4 servings

Easy Oven Beef Stew

2 pounds boneless beef stew meat, cut into 1½-inch cubes
1 can (16 ounces) tomatoes, undrained, cut up
1 can (10½ ounces) condensed beef broth
1 cup HOLLAND HOUSE® Red Cooking Wine
6 potatoes, peeled, quartered
6 carrots, cut into 2-inch pieces
3 ribs celery, cut into 1-inch pieces
2 medium onions, peeled, quartered
⅓ cup instant tapioca
1 tablespoon dried Italian seasoning*
¼ teaspoon black pepper
Chopped fresh parsley

*You can substitute 1½ teaspoons each of dried basil and oregano for Italian seasoning.

Heat oven to 325°F. Combine all ingredients except parsley in ovenproof Dutch oven; cover. Bake 2½ to 3 hours or until meat and vegetables are tender. Garnish with parsley. *Makes 8 servings*

Olive Sauce Pasta Shells with Chicken

1 jar (26 ounces) BARILLA® Green and Black Olive Pasta Sauce
2 cups chopped cooked chicken
½ cup (2 ounces) grated Parmesan cheese, divided
2 tablespoons capers, drained
1 package (16 ounces) BARILLA® Medium Shells

1. Combine pasta sauce, chicken, ¼ cup cheese and capers in large saucepan. Cook over medium heat 10 minutes, stirring occasionally.

2. Meanwhile, cook shells according to package directions; drain. Transfer to large platter.

3. Pour pasta sauce mixture over hot drained shells; sprinkle with remaining ¼ cup cheese.   *Makes 8 to 10 servings*

Note: For 2 cups chopped cooked chicken use ¾ pound boneless, skinless chicken breasts. To save time, purchase a rotisserie chicken or packaged (frozen) cooked chicken from the supermarket.

BEST WAY TO COOK PASTA
To cook pasta perfectly you need plenty of rapidly boiling salted water—4 to 6 quarts for 1 pound of pasta. Cook pasta at a full boil and stir occasionally for even cooking and to prevent sticking. Check doneness at minimum suggested time by removing a piece and tasting.

Golden Glazed Flank Steak

1 envelope LIPTON® RECIPE SECRETS® Onion Soup Mix*
1 jar (12 ounces) apricot or peach preserves
½ cup water
1 beef flank steak (about 2 pounds), cut into thin strips
2 medium green, red and/or yellow bell peppers, sliced
  Hot cooked rice

*Also terrific with LIPTON® RECIPE SECRETS® Onion-Mushroom Soup Mix.

1. In small bowl, combine soup mix, preserves and water; set aside.

2. On heavy-duty aluminum foil or in bottom of broiler pan with rack removed, arrange steak and green peppers; top with soup mixture.

3. Broil, turning steak and vegetables once, until steak is done. Serve over hot rice. *Makes 8 servings*

Easy Chicken and Potato Dinner

1 package (2 pounds) bone-in chicken breasts or thighs
1 pound potatoes, cut into wedges
½ cup KRAFT® Zesty Italian Dressing
1 tablespoon Italian seasoning
½ cup KRAFT® 100% Grated Parmesan Cheese

• **PLACE** chicken and potatoes in 13×9-inch baking pan.

• **POUR** dressing over chicken and potatoes. Sprinkle evenly with Italian seasoning and cheese.

• **BAKE** at 400°F for 1 hour or until chicken is cooked through and juices run clear. *Makes 4 servings*

Golden Glazed Flank Steak

Double Cheese Veal Cutlets

- 2 tablespoons butter
- 1 pound veal cutlets
  Salt and black pepper
- 4 cups CLAMATO® Tomato Cocktail
  Pinch of thyme
- 2 tablespoons grated Parmesan cheese
- 1 cup (4 ounces) shredded Swiss cheese
- 1 avocado, peeled and sliced

1. In large skillet, melt butter. Brown cutlets a few at a time, 2 minutes on each side. Remove and sprinkle lightly with salt and pepper.

2. Return veal to skillet, overlapping cutlets. Add Clamato and thyme; simmer 5 to 10 minutes, or until veal is tender. Arrange veal in ovenproof serving dish and pour sauce over veal. Sprinkle with Parmesan cheese and Swiss cheese. Place under preheated broiler 5 minutes, or until cheese is melted. Top cutlets with avocado slices.

Makes 6 to 8 servings

86

Cornish Veracruz

4 TYSON® Rock Cornish Game Hens (fresh or frozen, thawed)
1 cup cooked UNCLE BEN'S® ORIGINAL CONVERTED® Brand Rice
   Dried oregano, salt and black pepper to taste
½ cup olive oil
½ cup lime juice
 1 onion, diced
 1 cup chopped canned tomatoes
½ cup shredded Monterey Jack cheese
¼ cup sour cream
 1 tablespoon dried oregano leaves
 1 tablespoon capers
 1 teaspoon garlic powder
 1 teaspoon black pepper
½ teaspoon ground cumin

PREP: Preheat oven to 450°F. CLEAN: Wash hands. Sprinkle hens inside and out with oregano, salt and pepper. Combine oil and lime juice. Generously coat hens with mixture. Mix together remaining ingredients. Stuff into cavity of hens and truss. Place in greased roasting pan. CLEAN: Wash hands.

COOK: Bake 15 minutes. Reduce oven temperature to 375°F. Bake, basting occasionally with oil mixture, 30 to 45 minutes or until juices of hens run clear. (Or insert instant-read meat thermometer in thickest part of hen. Temperature should read 180°F.)

SERVE: Serve with black beans, if desired.

CHILL: Refrigerate leftovers immediately.   *Makes 8 servings*

Prep Time: 15 minutes
Cook Time: 45 to 60 minutes

Fettuccine with Squash, Peppers and Shrimp

1 package (16 ounces) uncooked BARILLA® fettuccine
2 tablespoons olive oil
½ cup sliced zucchini (¼-inch rounds)
½ cup sliced yellow squash (¼-inch rounds)
½ cup yellow bell pepper strips
1 pound medium shrimp, peeled
1 jar (26 ounces) BARILLA® Tomato & Basil Sauce
Chopped fresh basil and crushed red pepper, for garnish

Prepare fettuccine according to package directions; drain.

Heat oil in medium skillet over medium heat. Add zucchini, squash and bell pepper; cook 7 minutes or just until tender. Add shrimp and cook until pink and opaque. Add BARILLA® sauce; cook until heated through.

Add sauce mixture to cooked fettuccine in large bowl and toss well. Garnish with basil and crushed red pepper, if desired. Serve immediately. *Makes 4 to 6 servings*

Sirloin Steak Monte Carlo

   2 tablespoons olive or vegetable oil
1¾ pounds sirloin steak
   ½ cup sliced onion
   1 large clove garlic, minced
   ¼ cup pine nuts
   1 can (14.5 ounces) CONTADINA® Italian-Style Stewed Tomatoes, undrained
   2 tablespoons capers
   ½ teaspoon dried oregano leaves, crushed
   ½ teaspoon dried basil leaves, crushed
   ¼ teaspoon crushed red pepper flakes

1. Heat oil in large skillet over medium-high heat. Add steak; cook 4 to 5 minutes on each side for medium-rare.

2. Remove steak to platter, reserving any drippings in skillet; cover steak with foil to keep warm.

3. Add onion, garlic and pine nuts to skillet; sauté 5 minutes or until onion is tender and nuts are lightly toasted.

4. Add undrained tomatoes, capers, oregano, basil and red pepper flakes; simmer, uncovered, 5 minutes. Serve over steak.

Makes 4 to 6 servings

Sirloin Steak Monte Carlo

Jambalaya

1 pound large shrimp, shelled and deveined
½ pound kielbasa or smoked sausage, sliced
2 ribs celery, diagonally sliced
1 green bell pepper, cut into strips
1 can (14½ ounces) whole tomatoes, undrained
1 can (10½ ounces) condensed chicken broth
2 tablespoons *Frank's® RedHot®* Cayenne Pepper Sauce
½ teaspoon dried thyme leaves
1⅓ cups uncooked instant rice
1⅓ cups *French's®* French Fried Onions, divided

Generously spray large nonstick skillet with nonstick cooking spray; heat over high heat. Add shrimp and sausage; cook about 3 minutes or until shrimp are opaque.

Stir in celery, bell pepper, tomatoes with liquid, chicken broth, **Frank's RedHot** Sauce, thyme, rice and ⅔ cup French Fried Onions. Bring to a boil, stirring occasionally. Cover; remove from heat. Let stand 5 to 8 minutes or until all liquid is absorbed. Sprinkle with remaining ⅔ cup onions just before serving.   *Makes 6 servings*

Prep Time: 10 minutes
Cook Time: 10 minutes

Lamb Chops with Fresh Herbs

⅓ **cup red wine vinegar**
⅓ **cup vegetable oil**
 2 **tablespoons soy sauce**
 2 **tablespoons sherry**
 1 **tablespoon lemon juice**
 1 **tablespoon LAWRY'S® Seasoned Salt**
 1 **teaspoon LAWRY'S® Garlic Powder with Parsley**
 1 **teaspoon chopped fresh oregano**
 1 **teaspoon chopped fresh rosemary**
 1 **teaspoon chopped fresh thyme**
 1 **teaspoon chopped fresh marjoram**
 1 **teaspoon dry mustard**
½ **teaspoon white pepper**
 8 **lamb loin chops (about 2 pounds), cut 1 inch thick**

In large resealable plastic food storage bag, combine all ingredients except chops; mix well. Remove ½ cup marinade for basting. Add chops; seal bag. Marinate in refrigerator at least 1 hour. Remove chops from marinade; discard used marinade. Grill or broil chops until desired doneness, about 8 minutes, turning once and basting often with remaining ½ cup marinade. *Do not baste during last 5 minutes of cooking.* Discard any remaining marinade.   *Makes 4 to 6 servings*

Serving Suggestion: Serve with mashed potatoes and fresh green beans.

Hint: Substitute ¼ to ½ teaspoon dried herbs for each teaspoon of fresh herbs.

Grilled Beef with Two Sauces

1 (1-pound) boneless beef sirloin steak

ROASTED GARLIC SAUCE
¾ **cup mayonnaise**
¼ **cup Roasted Garlic Purée (recipe follows)**
¼ **cup GREY POUPON® Dijon Mustard**
1 **tablespoon lemon juice**
2 **tablespoons chopped parsley**

SUNDRIED TOMATO SAUCE
¾ **cup chopped roasted red peppers**
½ **cup sundried tomatoes,* chopped**
3 **tablespoons GREY POUPON® Dijon Mustard**
2 **tablespoons chopped parsley**
2 **to 3 tablespoons olive oil**
¼ **teaspoon crushed red pepper flakes**

*If sundried tomatoes are very dry, soften in warm water for 15 minutes. Drain before using.

1. Grill beef over medium heat to desired doneness and refrigerate.

2. For Roasted Garlic Sauce, blend all ingredients in medium bowl. Refrigerate at least 1 hour to blend flavors.

3. For Sundried Tomato Sauce, combine roasted red peppers, sundried tomatoes, mustard and parsley in medium bowl. Slowly add oil as needed to bind. Add red pepper flakes. Refrigerate at least 1 hour to blend flavors. Bring to room temperature before serving.

4. Slice beef and arrange on 4 serving plates. Spoon about 2 tablespoons of each sauce onto each plate. Serve with sliced tomatoes and cooled steamed asparagus; garnish as desired.

Makes 4 servings

Roasted Garlic Purée: Remove excess papery skin of 1 head garlic and separate into cloves. Place in 8×8×2-inch baking pan. Add 2 to 3 tablespoons olive oil and 1 cup chicken broth. Bake at 350°F for 25 to 30 minutes or until garlic is soft. Cool and squeeze garlic pulp from skins; discard liquid in pan.

Party Stuffed Pinwheels

1 envelope LIPTON® RECIPE SECRETS® Savory Herb with Garlic Soup Mix*
1 package (8 ounces) cream cheese, softened
1 cup shredded mozzarella cheese (about 4 ounces)
1 tablespoon grated Parmesan cheese
2 tablespoons milk
2 packages (10 ounces each) refrigerated pizza crust

Also terrific with LIPTON® RECIPE SECRETS® Onion Soup Mix.

1. Preheat oven to 425°F. In medium bowl, combine all ingredients except pizza crusts; set aside.

2. Unroll pizza crusts, then top evenly with filling. Roll, starting at longest side, jelly-roll style. Cut into 32 rounds.**

3. On baking sheet sprayed with nonstick cooking spray, arrange rounds cut side down.

4. Bake uncovered 13 minutes or until golden brown.

Makes 32 pinwheels

**If rolled pizza crust is too soft to cut, refrigerate or freeze until firm.*

BEST WAY TO SOFTEN CREAM CHEESE
The microwave oven was made for tasks like this. To soften cream cheese quickly, remove it from its wrapper and place it in a medium microwavable bowl. Microwave at MEDIUM (50%) 15 to 20 seconds or until slightly softened.

99

Champagne Scallops & Asparagus

10 large cloves garlic, peeled and halved
 2 tablespoons I CAN'T BELIEVE IT'S NOT BUTTER!® Spread
20 large sea scallops, rinsed and dried
 ¼ cup apple juice or cider
 ¼ cup chopped shallots or onion
 ¼ cup dry champagne or white wine
 1 tablespoon pure maple syrup or pancake syrup
 4 tablespoons finely chopped chives, divided
   Hot cooked rice
 1 pound asparagus, cooked
 1 tablespoon lemon juice

In small saucepan, cover garlic with water and bring to a boil over high heat. Boil 5 minutes. Drain garlic and set aside.

In 12-inch skillet, melt I Can't Believe It's Not Butter! Spread over medium heat and cook 1 minute or until lightly golden. Add scallops and cook, stirring occasionally, 4 minutes or until scallops are opaque. Remove scallops and set aside.

In same skillet, stir in juice, shallots, champagne, maple syrup, garlic and 2 tablespoons chives. Bring to a boil over high heat. Continue boiling, scraping up any brown bits from bottom of skillet, until slightly thickened, about 2 minutes. On serving platter, arrange scallops over hot rice. Top with sauce and remaining chives. Serve with asparagus tossed with lemon juice. If desired season with salt and ground black pepper.   *Makes 4 servings*

Manicotti Marinara

1 package (8 ounces) BARILLA® Manicotti or ½ package (8 ounces)
   BARILLA® Jumbo Shells
2 jars (26 ounces each) BARILLA® Marinara Pasta Sauce, divided
2 eggs
1 container (15 ounces) ricotta cheese
4 cups (16 ounces) shredded mozzarella cheese, divided
1 cup (4 ounces) grated Parmesan cheese, divided
¼ cup chopped fresh parsley or 1 tablespoon dried parsley

1. Cook manicotti shells according to package directions; drain. Preheat oven to 350°F. Spray bottom of 15×10×2-inch glass baking dish with nonstick cooking spray. Spread 1 jar marinara sauce over bottom of baking dish.

2. Beat eggs in large bowl. Stir in ricotta, 3 cups mozzarella, ¾ cup Parmesan and parsley. Fill each cooked shell with ricotta mixture. Arrange filled shells in baking dish over sauce. Top with second jar of marinara sauce, remaining 1 cup mozzarella and ¼ cup Parmesan.

3. Cover with foil and bake about 45 minutes or until bubbly. Uncover and continue baking about 5 minutes or until cheese is melted. Let stand 5 minutes before serving.   *Makes 6 servings*

Note: One package (10 ounces) frozen chopped spinach, thawed and well drained, may be added to the ricotta mixture.

Crab-Stuffed Chicken Breasts

1 package (8 ounces) cream cheese, softened
6 ounces frozen crabmeat or imitation crabmeat, thawed and
    drained
1 envelope LIPTON® RECIPE SECRETS® Savory Herb with Garlic Soup
    Mix
6 boneless, skinless chicken breast halves (about 1½ pounds)
¼ cup all-purpose flour
2 eggs, beaten
¾ cup plain dry bread crumbs
2 tablespoons BERTOLLI® Olive Oil
1 tablespoon I CAN'T BELIEVE IT'S NOT BUTTER!® Spread

Preheat oven to 350°F. Combine cream cheese, crabmeat and soup
mix; set aside. With knife parallel to cutting board, slice horizontally
through each chicken breast, stopping 1 inch from opposite edge;
open breasts. Evenly spread each breast with cream cheese mixture.
Close each chicken breast, securing open edge with wooden
toothpicks.

Dip chicken in flour, then eggs, then bread crumbs, coating well. In
12-inch skillet, heat oil (over medium-high heat) and I Can't Believe It's
Not Butter!® Spread and cook chicken 10 minutes or until golden,
turning once. Transfer chicken to 13×9-inch baking dish and bake
uncovered 15 minutes or until chicken is no longer pink in center.
Remove toothpicks before serving.   *Makes about 6 servings*

Menu Suggestion: Serve with a mixed green salad and warm garlic
bread.

Wild Rice Shrimp Paella

1½ cups canned chicken broth
2 tablespoons butter or margarine
¹⁄₁₆ teaspoon saffron *or* ⅛ teaspoon turmeric
2 boxes UNCLE BEN'S® Butter & Herb Fast Cook Recipe Long Grain
   & Wild Rice
1 pound medium shrimp, peeled and deveined
1 can (14½ ounces) diced tomatoes, undrained
1 cup frozen green peas, thawed
2 jars (6 ounces each) marinated artichoke hearts, drained

1. Combine broth, butter, saffron and contents of seasoning packets, reserving rice, in large saucepan. Bring to a boil.

2. Add shrimp; cook over medium-high heat 2 minutes or until shrimp turn pink. Remove shrimp with slotted spoon and set aside.

3. Add tomatoes and reserved rice. Bring to a boil. Cover; reduce heat and simmer 15 minutes.

4. Stir in peas; cover and cook 5 minutes. Add artichoke hearts and shrimp; cover and cook 5 minutes or until hot and rice is tender. Let stand 3 minutes before serving. *Makes 6 servings*

BEST WAY TO PEEL AND DEVEIN SHRIMP
Start peeling shrimp at the large end. Peel away the shell from the underside (where the legs are). To devein, use a sharp knife to cut a very shallow slit down the middle of the outside curve of the shrimp. Pull out the dark vein with the tip of the knife, and rinse off the shrimp.

Coq au Vin

4 thin slices bacon, cut into ½-inch pieces
¾ teaspoon dried thyme leaves
6 chicken thighs, skinned
1 large onion, coarsely chopped
4 cloves garlic, minced
½ pound small red potatoes, cut into quarters
10 mushrooms, cut into quarters
1 can (14½ ounces) DEL MONTE® Diced Tomatoes with Garlic & Onion
1½ cups dry red wine

1. Cook bacon in 4-quart heavy saucepan until just starting to brown. Sprinkle chicken with thyme; season with salt and pepper, if desired.

2. Add chicken to pan; brown over medium-high heat. Add onion and garlic. Cook 2 minutes; drain.

3. Add potatoes, mushrooms, undrained tomatoes and wine. Cook, uncovered, over medium-high heat, stirring occasionally, about 25 minutes or until potatoes are tender, juices of chicken run clear and sauce thickens. Garnish with chopped parsley, if desired.

Makes 4 to 6 servings

Prep and Cook Time: 45 minutes

BEST WAY TO CLEAN MUSHROOMS
Mushrooms are like little sponges. They readily absorb liquid and become soggy if you soak them. To clean them, wipe with a damp paper towel. If mushrooms are unusually dirty and wiping isn't enough, rinse quickly under cold running water and blot dry with paper towels.

Pork Chops with Apple-Sage Stuffing

- 6 center-cut pork chops (3 pounds), about 1 inch thick
- ¾ cup dry vermouth, divided
- 4 tablespoons minced fresh sage *or* 4 teaspoons rubbed sage, divided
- 2 tablespoons soy sauce
- 1 tablespoon olive oil
- 2 cloves garlic, minced
- ½ teaspoon black pepper, divided
- 1 tablespoon butter
- 1 medium onion, diced
- 1 apple, cored and diced
- ½ teaspoon salt
- 2 cups fresh firm-textured white bread crumbs
  - Curly endive
  - Plum slices

Cut pocket in each chop using tip of thin, sharp knife. Combine ¼ cup vermouth, 2 tablespoons fresh sage (or 2 teaspoons rubbed sage), soy sauce, oil, garlic and ¼ teaspoon pepper in glass dish; add pork chops, turning to coat. Heat butter in large skillet over medium heat until foamy. Add onion and apple; cook and stir about 6 minutes until onion is tender. Stir in remaining ½ cup vermouth, 2 tablespoons sage, ¼ teaspoon pepper and salt. Cook and stir over high heat about 3 minutes until liquid is almost gone. Transfer onion mixture to large bowl. Stir in bread crumbs.

Remove pork chops from marinade; discard marinade. Spoon onion mixture into pockets of pork chops. Close openings with wooden picks. (Soak wooden picks in hot water 15 minutes to prevent burning.) Grill pork chops on covered grill over medium KINGSFORD® Briquets about 5 minutes per side until barely pink in center. Garnish with endive and plum slices. *Makes 6 servings*

GREAT GO–WITHS

Stuffed Portobello Mushrooms

- **1 box UNCLE BEN'S® Long Grain & Wild Rice Roasted Garlic**
- **2 tablespoons prepared pesto sauce**
- **8 ounces cream cheese, softened**
- **4 large portobello mushrooms**
  Salt and black pepper to taste
- **1 large tomato**
- **4 tablespoons grated Parmesan cheese**
- **4 basil leaves (optional)**

COOK: Preheat oven to 400°F. CLEAN: Wash hands. Prepare rice according to package directions. Meanwhile, stir pesto into cream cheese until well blended. Remove stems from mushrooms. Clean mushroom caps well. Place mushrooms, stem side up, on baking sheet. Sprinkle with salt and pepper. Spread one-fourth of cream cheese mixture onto each mushroom. Top with ½ cup cooked rice. Slice tomato into 4 thick slices. Place 1 slice on top of rice and sprinkle each mushroom with 1 tablespoon Parmesan cheese. Bake 10 minutes.

SERVE: Garnish each mushroom with basil leaf, if desired.

CHILL: Refrigerate leftovers immediately.

Makes 4 servings

Prep Time: none
Cook Time: 30 minutes

112

Great American Potato Salad

¾ **cup MIRACLE WHIP® Salad Dressing**
 1 **teaspoon KRAFT® Pure Prepared Mustard**
½ **teaspoon celery seed**
½ **teaspoon salt**
⅛ **teaspoon pepper**
 4 **cups cubed cooked potatoes**
 2 **hard-cooked eggs, chopped**
½ **cup chopped onion**
½ **cup celery slices**
½ **cup chopped sweet pickle**

• MIX salad dressing, mustard and seasonings in large bowl. Add remaining ingredients; mix lightly. Cover; refrigerate several hours or until chilled. *Makes 6 servings*

Prep Time: 15 minutes plus refrigerating

BEST WAY TO BOIL POTATOES
Choose new potatoes or boiling potatoes for salad making. Avoid russets as they tend to fall apart when cooked. Scrub potatoes well and leave skins on for best flavor and nutrition. Place them in a large saucepan and cover with water by 1 inch. Boil until tender (about 25 minutes for medium potatoes). If you want to remove the peels, do it when the potatoes are still warm and the skin comes off easily.

Tortellini Soup

3 cloves garlic, minced
1 tablespoon butter or margarine
1 can (48 ounces) COLLEGE INN ® Chicken or Beef Broth
1 package (about 19 ounces) frozen cheese tortellini
1 package (10 ounces) frozen chopped spinach, thawed
2 cans (14½ ounces each) stewed tomatoes, undrained, cut into
    pieces
Grated Parmesan cheese

In large saucepan, over medium-high heat cook garlic in butter for
1 to 2 minutes. Add broth and tortellini. Heat to a boil; reduce heat
and simmer 10 minutes. Add spinach and tomatoes; simmer 5 minutes
longer. Sprinkle each serving with cheese.

Makes 8 to 10 servings (about 11 cups)

Vegetables Italiano

1 cup Italian-seasoned bread crumbs
⅓ cup grated Parmesan cheese
⅔ cup HELLMANN'S® or BEST FOODS® Real or Light Mayonnaise or
    Low Fat Mayonnaise Dressing
6 cups assorted vegetables: broccoli florets, carrot slices,
    cauliflower florets, small mushrooms, green and/or red bell
    pepper strips, yellow squash slices and/or zucchini strips

1. Preheat oven to 425°F.

2. In plastic food bag combine crumbs and Parmesan; shake to blend
well. In another bag combine mayonnaise and vegetables; shake to
coat well. Add mayonnaise-coated vegetables, half at a time, to crumb
mixture; shake to coat well.

3. Arrange in single layer on ungreased cookie sheet so that pieces do
not touch.

4. Bake in 425°F oven 10 minutes or until golden.

Makes about 8 servings

Grilled Sweet Potatoes

4 medium-sized sweet potatoes (2 pounds), peeled
⅓ cup *French's®* Napa Valley Style Dijon Mustard
2 tablespoons olive oil
1 tablespoon minced fresh rosemary *or* 1 teaspoon dried rosemary
½ teaspoon salt
¼ teaspoon black pepper

1. Cut potatoes diagonally into ½-inch-thick slices. Place potatoes and 1 cup water in shallow microwavable dish. Cover with vented plastic wrap and microwave on HIGH (100%) 6 minutes or until potatoes are crisp-tender, turning once. (Cook potatoes in two batches, if necessary.) Drain well.

2. Combine mustard, oil, rosemary, salt and pepper in small bowl; brush on potato slices. Place potatoes on oiled grid. Grill over medium-high heat 5 to 8 minutes or until potatoes are fork-tender, turning and basting often with mustard mixture.   *Makes 4 servings*

Prep Time: 15 minutes
Cook Time: 18 minutes

BEST WAY TO CHOOSE SWEET POTATOES
Look for medium-sized potatoes with thick, dark orange skins that are free from bruises. Sweet potatoes keep best in a dry, dark area at about 55°F. Under these conditions they should last about 3 to 4 weeks.

Grilled Sweet Potatoes

Juicy Layered Orange Pineapple Mold

1 can (20 ounces) crushed pineapple in juice, undrained
Cold orange juice
1½ cups boiling water
1 package (8-serving size) *or* 2 packages (4-serving size each)
JELL-O® Brand Orange Flavor Gelatin
1 package (8 ounces) PHILADELPHIA® Cream Cheese, softened

DRAIN pineapple, reserving juice. Add cold orange juice to pineapple juice to make 1½ cups. Stir boiling water into gelatin in large bowl at least 2 minutes until completely dissolved. Stir in measured juice. Reserve 1 cup gelatin at room temperature.

STIR ½ of the crushed pineapple into remaining gelatin. Pour into 6-cup mold which has been sprayed with no stick cooking spray. Refrigerate about 2 hours or until set but not firm (should stick to finger when touched and should mound).

STIR reserved gelatin gradually into cream cheese in medium bowl with wire whisk until smooth. Stir in remaining crushed pineapple. Spoon over gelatin layer in mold.

REFRIGERATE 4 hours or until firm. Unmold. Garnish as desired.

Makes 10 servings

Prep Time: 20 minutes
RefrigerateTime: 6 hours

BEST WAY TO UNMOLD GELATIN
Use moistened fingertips to gently pull the gelatin away from the edges of the mold. Dip the mold into a large bowl of warm water for 10 seconds. Cover the mold with a serving plate and invert. Give the mold a gentle shake or two. If it does not slide out at once, return it to the bowl of water for a few seconds.

Chicken Caesar Salad

1 package BUTTERBALL® Chicken Breast Tenders
¼ cup prepared Caesar salad dressing
½ teaspoon minced garlic
6 cups torn romaine lettuce
1 large tomato, cut into wedges
1½ cups Caesar-flavored croutons
½ cup shredded Parmesan cheese
Anchovy fillets, optional

Combine chicken, salad dressing and garlic in large skillet. Cook over medium-high heat 4 to 5 minutes or until chicken is no longer pink in center, turning frequently to brown evenly. Divide romaine lettuce among 4 plates. Top with tomato and croutons. Arrange chicken tenders on top of each salad. Sprinkle with Parmesan cheese; top with anchovy fillets, if desired. Serve with additional salad dressing.
Makes 4 servings

Preparation Time: 15 minutes

BEST ADVICE ON ANCHOVIES
If you like the flavor of anchovy, but don't want to use whole canned fillets, try adding a bit of anchovy paste to prepared Caesar dressing (½ teaspoon paste is equal to 1 fillet). You can also make your own paste by crushing anchovy fillets in a bowl with a fork.

Parker House Rolls

4¾ to 5¼ cups all-purpose flour, divided
⅓ cup sugar
2 envelopes FLEISCHMANN'S® RapidRise™ Yeast
1½ teaspoons salt
¾ cup milk
¾ cup water
¼ cup butter or margarine
1 large egg
¼ cup butter or margarine, melted

In large bowl, combine 2 cups flour, sugar, undissolved yeast and salt. Heat milk, water and ¼ cup butter until very warm (120° to 130°F). Stir into dry ingredients. Beat 2 minutes at medium speed of electric mixer, scraping bowl occasionally. Add egg and ½ cup flour; beat 2 minutes at high speed. Stir in enough remaining flour to make a soft dough. Knead on lightly floured surface until smooth and elastic, about 8 to 10 minutes. Cover*; let rest 10 minutes.

Divide dough in half; roll each half into 12-inch square, about ¼ inch thick. Cut each into 6 (12×2-inch) strips. Cut each strip into 3 (4×2-inch) rectangles. Brush each rectangle with melted butter. Crease length of rectangles slightly off center with dull edge of knife and fold at crease. Arrange rolls side by side in rows, slightly overlapping, on greased baking sheets, with shorter side of each roll facing down. Allow ¼ inch of space between each row. Cover; let rise in warm, draft-free place until doubled in size, about 30 minutes.

Bake at 400°F for 13 to 15 minutes or until done. Remove from sheets; cool on wire rack. Brush with remaining melted butter.

Makes 36 rolls

If desired, allow dough to rise in refrigerator 12 to 24 hours.

Mexican Taco Salad

    1 pound ground beef or turkey
    1 cup (1 small) chopped onion
    1 cup ORTEGA® Salsa Prima-Thick & Chunky Mild
    ¾ cup water
    1 package (1¼ ounces) ORTEGA® Taco Seasoning Mix
  1¾ cups (15-ounce can) kidney or pinto beans, rinsed and drained
    ½ cup (4-ounce can) ORTEGA® Diced Green Chiles
    6 tortilla shells *or* 3 cups (3 ounces) tortilla chips
    6 cups shredded lettuce, *divided*
      Chopped tomatoes (optional)
    ¾ cup (3 ounces) shredded Nacho & Taco blend cheese, *divided*
      Sour cream (optional)
      Guacamole (optional)
      ORTEGA® Thick & Smooth Taco Sauce

COOK beef and onion until beef is brown; drain. Stir in salsa, water and seasoning mix. Bring to a boil. Reduce heat to low; cook for 2 to 3 minutes. Stir in beans and chiles.

LAYER ingredients as follows in *each* shell: *1 cup* lettuce, *¾ cup* meat mixture, tomatoes *2 tablespoons* cheese and sour cream. Serve with guacamole and taco sauce.   *Makes 6 servings*

Original Green Bean Casserole

> 1 can (10¾ ounces) condensed cream of mushroom soup
> ¾ cup milk
> ⅛ teaspoon ground black pepper
> 2 packages (9 ounces each) frozen cut green beans, thawed and
> drained *or* 2 cans (14½ ounces each) cut green beans, drained
> 1⅓ cups *French's*® French Fried Onions, divided

Preheat oven to 350°F. Combine soup, milk and ground pepper in
1½-quart casserole; stir until well blended. Stir in beans and ⅔ *cup*
French Fried Onions.

Bake, uncovered, 30 minutes or until hot. Stir; sprinkle with remaining
⅔ *cup* onions. Bake 5 minutes or until onions are golden.

Makes 6 servings

Microwave Directions: Prepare green bean mixture as above; pour
into 1½-quart microwave-safe casserole. Cook, covered, on HIGH 8 to
10 minutes or until heated through. Stir beans halfway through
cooking time. Top with remaining French Fried Onions; cook,
uncovered, 1 minute. Let stand 5 minutes.

Prep Time: 5 minutes
Cook Time: 35 minutes

Easy Ham & Veg•All® Chowder

> 2 cans (15 ounces each) VEG•ALL® Original Mixed Vegetables, with
> liquid
> 1 can (10¾ ounces) cream of potato soup
> 1 cup cooked ham, cubed
> ½ teaspoon dried basil
> ¼ teaspoon black pepper

In medium saucepan, combine Veg•All, soup, ham, basil and black
pepper. Heat until hot; serve. *Makes 4 to 6 servings*

Prep Time: 7 minutes

Acorn Squash Filled with Savory Spinach

4 small acorn squash
2 tablespoons FILIPPO BERIO® Olive Oil
1 (10-ounce) package frozen chopped spinach, thawed and drained
1 (8-ounce) container ricotta cheese
1 tablespoon grated Parmesan cheese
¼ teaspoon freshly ground black pepper
⅛ teaspoon salt
⅛ teaspoon ground nutmeg

Preheat oven to 325°F. Cut squash crosswise in half. Scoop out seeds and fibers; discard. Brush insides and outsides of squash halves with olive oil. Place in large shallow roasting pan. Bake, uncovered, 35 to 40 minutes or until tender when pierced with fork.

In medium bowl, combine spinach, ricotta cheese, Parmesan cheese, pepper, salt and nutmeg. Spoon equal amounts of spinach mixture into squash halves. Bake, uncovered, an additional 10 to 15 minutes or until heated through. *Makes 8 servings*

To Microwave: Prepare squash as directed above. Place in large shallow microwave-safe dish. Cover with vented plastic wrap. Microwave on HIGH (100% power) 10 to 12 minutes or until squash are softened, rotating dish halfway through cooking. Prepare filling; spoon into squash halves. Cover with vented plastic wrap; microwave on HIGH 6 to 8 minutes or until filling is hot and squash are tender when pierced with fork.

Famous Crab Rice Salad

1 bag SUCCESS® Rice
1 package (6 ounces) frozen crabmeat, thawed
1 cup sliced celery
¾ cup chopped seeded tomato
½ cup chopped onion
¼ cup reduced-calorie mayonnaise
2 tablespoons cider vinegar
1 tablespoon olive oil
1 tablespoon hot pepper sauce
1 tablespoon Dijon mustard
1 clove garlic, minced
½ teaspoon salt
½ teaspoon dried basil leaves, crushed

Prepare rice according to package directions. Cool.

Place rice in large bowl. Add crabmeat, celery, tomato, onion and mayonnaise; mix lightly. Combine vinegar, oil, hot pepper sauce, mustard, garlic, salt and basil in jar with tight-fitting lid; shake well. Pour over rice mixture; toss gently to coat. Refrigerate 2 hours. Garnish, if desired.   *Makes 6 to 8 servings*

BEST TIPS ON CRABMEAT
Always pick over crabmeat carefully to make sure there are no tiny pieces of shell or cartilage. When substituting canned crabmeat for frozen, taste it first. If there is a metallic flavor, soak it in ice water for 5 minutes. Then drain and blot dry. Crabmeat is very perishable, so plan on using refrigerated leftovers within 2 days.

Velveeta® Spicy Southwest Corn Cheese Soup

1 package (10 ounces) frozen sweet corn, thawed, drained
1 clove garlic, minced
1 tablespoon butter or margarine
¾ pound (12 ounces) VELVEETA® Pasteurized Prepared Cheese Product, cut up
1 can (4 ounces) chopped green chilies
¾ cup chicken broth
¾ cup milk
2 tablespoons chopped fresh cilantro

1. Cook and stir corn and garlic in butter in large saucepan on medium-high heat until tender. Reduce heat to medium.

2. Stir in remaining ingredients; cook until VELVEETA is melted and soup is thoroughly heated. Top each serving with crushed tortilla chips, if desired. *Makes 4 (1-cup) servings*

Prep Time: 15 minutes
Cook Time: 10 minutes

Manhattan Clam Chowder

  2 pieces bacon, diced
  1 large red bell pepper, diced
  1 large green bell pepper, diced
  1 rib celery, chopped
  1 carrot, peeled and chopped
  1 small onion, chopped
  1 clove garlic, finely chopped
  2 cups bottled clam juice
  1 cup CLAMATO® Tomato Cocktail
  2 medium potatoes, peeled and diced
  1 large tomato, chopped
  1 teaspoon oregano
  ½ teaspoon black pepper
  2 cups fresh or canned clams, chopped (about 24 shucked clams)

In heavy 4-quart saucepan, sauté bacon, peppers, celery, carrot, onion and garlic over medium heat until tender, about 10 minutes. (Do not brown bacon.) Add clam juice, Clamato, potatoes, tomato, oregano and pepper. Simmer 35 minutes or until potatoes are tender. Add clams; cook 5 minutes more.   *Makes 8 servings*

Pineapple Boats with Citrus Creme

1 large DOLE® Fresh Pineapple
1 DOLE® Banana, peeled, sliced
1 orange, peeled, sliced
1 apple, cored, sliced
1 DOLE® Pear, cored, sliced
1 cup seedless DOLE® Grapes (red and green)

CITRUS CREME
1 cup plain nonfat yogurt
2 tablespoons brown sugar
1 tablespoon minced crystallized ginger, optional
1 teaspoon grated orange peel
1 teaspoon grated lime peel

• Cut pineapple in half lengthwise through the crown. Cut fruit from shells, leaving shells intact. Core and chunk fruit.

• Combine pineapple chunks with remaining fruit. Spoon into pineapple boats.

• Combine all ingredients for Citrus Creme. Serve with pineapple boats   *Makes 8 servings*

Prep Time: 20 minutes

Chocolate Lava Cakes

6 tablespoons I CAN'T BELIEVE IT'S NOT BUTTER!® Spread
3 squares (1 ounce each) bittersweet or semi-sweet chocolate, cut into pieces
½ cup granulated sugar
6 tablespoons all-purpose flour
    Pinch salt
2 large eggs
2 large egg yolks
¼ teaspoon vanilla extract
    Confectioners' sugar

Line bottom of four (4-ounce) ramekins or custard cups with waxed paper, then grease; set aside.

In medium microwave-safe bowl, microwave I Can't Believe It's Not Butter! Spread and chocolate at HIGH (Full Power) 45 seconds or until chocolate is melted; stir until smooth. With wire whisk, beat in granulated sugar, flour and salt. Beat in eggs, egg yolks and vanilla. Spoon into prepared ramekins. Refrigerate 1 hour or until ready to bake.

Preheat oven to 425°F. Bake 13 minutes or until edges are firm but centers are still slightly soft. On wire rack, cool 5 minutes. Run sharp knife around cake edges. Unmold onto serving plates, and remove waxed paper. Sprinkle with confectioners' sugar and serve immediately.

Makes 4 servings

138

Hot Chocolate Soufflé

¾ **cup HERSHEY'S Cocoa**
1 **cup sugar, divided**
½ **cup all-purpose flour**
¼ **teaspoon salt**
2 **cups milk**
6 **egg yolks, well beaten**
2 **tablespoons butter or margarine**
1 **teaspoon vanilla extract**
8 **egg whites**
¼ **teaspoon cream of tartar**
  Sweetened whipped cream

1. Adjust oven rack to lowest position. Heat oven to 350°F. Lightly butter 2½-quart soufflé dish; sprinkle with sugar. For collar, cut a length of heavy-duty aluminum foil to fit around soufflé dish; fold in thirds lengthwise. Lightly butter one side of foil. Attach foil, buttered side in, around outside of dish, allowing foil to extend at least 2 inches above dish. Secure foil with tape or string.

2. Stir together cocoa, ¾ cup sugar, flour and salt in large saucepan; gradually stir in milk. Cook over medium heat, stirring constantly with wire whisk, until mixture boils; remove from heat. Stir small amount of chocolate mixture into egg yolks; blend well. Add egg mixture to chocolate mixture in pan, blending well. Cook and stir 1 minute. Blend in butter and vanilla. Cool 20 minutes.

3. Beat egg whites with cream of tartar in large bowl until soft peaks form; add remaining ¼ cup sugar, beating until stiff peaks form. Gently fold one third of beaten egg white mixture into chocolate mixture. Lightly fold chocolate mixture, half at a time, into remaining beaten egg white mixture just until blended; do not overfold.

4. Gently pour mixture into prepared dish; smooth top with spatula. Gently place dish in larger baking pan; pour hot water into larger pan to depth of 1 inch.

5. Bake 65 to 70 minutes or until puffed and set. Remove soufflé dish from water. Carefully remove foil. Serve immediately with sweetened whipped cream.   *Makes 8 to 10 servings*

Classic Boston Cream Pie

⅓ cup shortening
1 cup sugar
2 eggs
1 teaspoon vanilla extract
1¼ cups all-purpose flour
1½ teaspoons baking powder
¼ teaspoon salt
¾ cup milk
   Rich Filling (recipe page 144)
   Dark Cocoa Glaze (recipe page 144)

1. Heat oven to 350°F. Grease and flour 9-inch round baking pan.

2. Beat shortening, sugar, eggs and vanilla in large bowl until fluffy. Stir together flour, baking powder and salt; add alternately with milk to shortening mixture, beating well after each addition. Pour batter into prepared pan.

3. Bake 30 to 35 minutes or until wooden pick inserted in center comes out clean. Cool 10 minutes; remove from pan to wire rack. Cool completely.

4. Prepare Rich Filling. With long serrated knife, cut cake in half horizontally. Place one layer, cut side up, on serving plate; spread with prepared filling. Top with remaining layer, cut side down. Prepare Dark Cocoa Glaze; spread over cake, allowing glaze to run down sides. Refrigerate several hours or until cold. Garnish as desired. Refrigerate leftover pie. *Makes 8 to 10 servings*

continued on page 144

Classic Boston Cream Pie

Classic Boston Cream Pie, continued

Rich Filling

⅓ **cup sugar**
2 **tablespoons cornstarch**
1½ **cups milk**
2 **egg yolks, slightly beaten**
1 **tablespoon butter or margarine**
1 **teaspoon vanilla extract**

Stir together sugar and cornstarch in medium saucepan; gradually add milk and egg yolks, stirring until blended. Cook over medium heat, stirring constantly, until mixture comes to a boil. Boil 1 minute, stirring constantly. Remove from heat; stir in butter and vanilla. Cover; refrigerate several hours or until cold.

Dark Cocoa Glaze

3 **tablespoons water**
2 **tablespoons butter or margarine**
3 **tablespoons HERSHEY'S Cocoa**
1 **cup powdered sugar**
½ **teaspoon vanilla extract**

Heat water and butter in small saucepan over medium heat until mixture comes to a boil; remove from heat. Immediately stir in cocoa. Gradually add powdered sugar and vanilla, beating with whisk until smooth and of desired consistency; cool slightly.

Makes about ¾ cup glaze

BEST TIP ON COCOA POWDER
Don't confuse the unsweetened cocoa powder called for in this recipe with the cocoa mix or instant cocoa used to make hot chocolate. Unsweetened cocoa powder is made by grinding the dried chocolate solids left after removing most of the cocoa butter from cocoa beans. Store cocoa in an airtight container in a cool dark place for up to two years.

Chocolate Mousse Espresso

2 envelopes KNOX® Unflavored Gelatine
¾ cup sugar, divided
4 teaspoons instant espresso coffee powder
2¾ cups milk
12 (1 ounce each) squares semisweet chocolate
1½ cups heavy cream
45 NABISCO® Famous Chocolate Wafers
⅔ cup hazelnuts, toasted

Combine gelatine with ½ cup sugar and coffee powder in medium saucepan. Stir in milk. Let stand without stirring 3 minutes for gelatine to soften. Heat over low heat, stirring constantly, until gelatine is completely dissolved, about 5 minutes.

Add chocolate and continue heating over low heat, stirring constantly, until chocolate is melted. Using wire whisk, beat until chocolate is thoroughly blended. Pour into large bowl and refrigerate, stirring occasionally, until mixture mounds slightly when dropped from spoon. Remove from refrigerator.

Pour chilled heavy cream and remaining ¼ cup sugar into chilled bowl and beat with electric mixer at high speed until soft peaks form. Reserve ½ cup for garnish.

Gently fold remaining whipped cream into gelatine mixture.

Place wafers and hazelnuts in food processor or blender container; process with on/off pulses until finely crushed.

Alternately layer gelatine mixture with cookie crumb mixture in dessert dishes. Refrigerate at least 30 minutes. Garnish, if desired.

Makes about 10 servings

Chocolate Mallow Cookie Pie

 2 cups JET-PUFFED® Miniature Marshmallows
 2 tablespoons milk
2½ cups thawed COOL WHIP® Whipped Topping
 2 cups cold milk
 2 packages (4-serving size) JELL-O® Chocolate Flavor Instant
    Pudding & Pie Filling
 1 OREO® Pie Crust (9 inch)
14 NILLA® wafers, chopped
    Chocolate Topping (recipe follows, optional)

MICROWAVE marshmallows and 2 tablespoons milk in medium microwavable bowl on HIGH 1 minute, stirring after 30 seconds. Stir until marshmallows are melted. Refrigerate 15 minutes to cool. Gently stir in 1 cup of the whipped topping.

POUR 2 cups milk into large bowl. Add pudding mixes. Beat with wire whisk 2 minutes or until well blended. Gently stir in remaining whipped topping. Spoon into crust. Arrange cookies over top. Spread marshmallow mixture over cookies. Drizzle with Chocolate Topping.

REFRIGERATE 4 hours or until set.   *Makes 8 servings*

Chocolate Topping: Microwave 2 squares BAKER'S® Semi-Sweet Baking Chocolate in heavy zipper-style plastic sandwich bag on HIGH 1 to 2 minutes or until chocolate is almost melted. Add 2 teaspoons softened butter; gently squeeze bag until chocolate and butter are completely melted. Fold down top of bag; snip tiny piece off 1 corner from bottom. Drizzle chocolate mixture over top of pie. Refrigerate as directed above.

Prep Time: 30 minutes plus refrigerating

Chocolate Intensity

CAKE
>   4 bars (8-ounce box) NESTLÉ® TOLL HOUSE® Unsweetened
>   Chocolate Baking Bars, broken into pieces
> ½ cup (1 stick) butter, softened
> 1½ cups granulated sugar
>   3 large eggs
>   2 teaspoons vanilla extract
> ⅔ cup all-purpose flour
>   Powdered sugar (optional)

COFFEE CRÈME ANGLAISE SAUCE
>   4 large egg yolks, lightly beaten
> ⅓ cup granulated sugar
>   1 tablespoon TASTER'S CHOICE® 100% Pure Instant Coffee
> 1½ cups milk
>   1 teaspoon vanilla extract

PREHEAT oven to 350°F. Grease 9-inch springform pan.

FOR CAKE
MICROWAVE baking bars in medium, microwave-safe bowl on HIGH (100%) power for 1 minute; stir. Microwave at additional 10- to 20-second intervals, stirring until smooth; cool to lukewarm.

BEAT butter, sugar, eggs and vanilla extract in small mixer bowl for about 4 minutes or until thick and pale yellow. Beat in chocolate; gradually beat in flour. Spread into prepared springform pan.

BAKE for 25 to 28 minutes or until wooden pick inserted in center comes out moist. Cool in pan on wire rack for 15 minutes. Loosen and remove side of pan; cool completely. Sprinkle with powdered sugar; serve with Coffee Crème Anglaise Sauce.

FOR COFFEE CRÈME ANGLAISE SAUCE
PLACE egg yolks in medium bowl. Combine sugar and Taster's Choice in saucepan; stir in milk. Cook over medium heat, stirring constantly, until mixture comes just to a simmer. Remove from heat. Gradually whisk *half* of milk into yolks; return mixture to saucepan. Cook, stirring constantly, for 3 to 4 minutes or until slightly thickened. Strain into bowl; stir in vanilla. Cover; refrigerate.   *Makes 10 to 12 Servings*

Chocolate Intensity

Chocolate Mayonnaise Cake

   2 cups all-purpose flour
   ⅔ cup unsweetened cocoa
   1¼ teaspoons baking soda
   ¼ teaspoon baking powder
   3 eggs
   1⅔ cups sugar
   1 teaspoon vanilla
   1 cup HELLMANN'S® or BEST FOODS® Real or Light Mayonnaise
   1⅓ cups water

1. Preheat oven to 350°F. Grease and flour bottoms of two 9×1½-inch round cake pans.

2. In medium bowl, combine flour, cocoa, baking soda and baking powder; set aside.

3. In large bowl with mixer at high speed, beat eggs, sugar and vanilla, scraping bowl occasionally, 3 minutes or until smooth and creamy. Reduce speed to low; beat in mayonnaise until blended. Add flour mixture in 4 additions alternately with water, beginning and ending with flour mixture. Pour into prepared pans.

4. Bake 30 to 35 minutes or until cake springs back when touched lightly in center. Cool in pans on wire racks 10 minutes. Remove from pans; cool completely on racks. Fill and frost as desired.

Makes 1 (9-inch) layer cake

Deep Dish Mocha Tiramisu

1 (14-ounce) can EAGLE® BRAND Sweetened Condensed Milk (NOT
   evaporated milk), divided
1 (18¼-ounce) package chocolate cake mix with pudding
1 cup water
2 large eggs
½ cup vegetable oil
   Creamy Coffee Filling (recipe page 154)
   Espresso Sauce (recipe page 154)
½ cup coffee liqueur
   Chocolate-covered coffee beans

1. Preheat oven to 350°F. Grease 5 (8-inch) round cake pans. Reserve ¼ cup Eagle Brand for Creamy Coffee Filling.

2. In large mixing bowl, beat remaining ¾ cup Eagle Brand, cake mix, water, eggs and oil until blended. Pour 1 cup batter into each prepared pan.

3. Bake 13 to 14 minutes. Cool in pans on wire racks 10 minutes. Remove from pans; cool completely on wire racks. Prepare Creamy Coffee Filling and Espresso Sauce.

4. Brush each cake layer evenly with liqueur. Place 1 cake layer in 4-quart trifle dish or bowl; top with 1½ cups Creamy Coffee Filling. Drizzle with ½ cup Espresso Sauce. Repeat procedure with remaining cake layers, 1 cup chocolate filling, and ¼ cup sauce, ending with cake layer. Garnish with chocolate-covered coffee beans. Chill. Store covered in refrigerator.   *Makes 12 servings*

Prep Time: 15 minutes
Bake Time: 13 to 14 minutes

continued on page 154

Deep Dish Mocha Tiramisu, continued

Creamy Coffee Filling

¼ cup reserved EAGLE® BRAND Sweetened Condensed Milk (NOT evaporated milk)
1 (8-ounce) package cream cheese, softened
2 tablespoons coffee liqueur
1½ cups whipping cream

In large mixing bowl, beat first 3 ingredients until blended, about 4 minutes. Add whipping cream and beat until stiff peaks form. Chill, if desired.   *Makes 4½ cups filling*

Prep Time: 10 minutes

Espresso Sauce

1 cup water
½ cup ground espresso
1 (14-ounce) can EAGLE® BRAND Sweetened Condensed Milk (NOT evaporated milk)
¼ cup (½ stick) butter or margarine

In small saucepan over medium heat, bring 1 cup water and ground espresso to a boil. Remove from heat and let stand 5 minutes. Pour mixture through fine wire-mesh strainer; discard grounds. In small saucepan over medium heat, combine espresso and Eagle Brand. Bring to a boil. Remove from heat, stir in butter. Cool.

Makes 1¼ cups sauce

Prep Time: 10 minutes

Oreo® Cheesecake

1 (20-ounce) package OREO® Chocolate Sandwich Cookies, divided
⅓ cup margarine or butter, melted
3 (8-ounce) packages cream cheese, softened
¾ cup sugar
4 eggs
1 cup sour cream
1 teaspoon vanilla
Whipped cream for garnish

1. Preheat oven to 350°F. Finely roll 30 cookies; coarsely chop 20 cookies. Mix finely rolled cookie crumbs and margarine or butter in medium bowl. Press on bottom and 2 inches up side of 9-inch springform pan; set aside.

2. Beat cream cheese and sugar in large bowl with electric mixer at medium speed until creamy. Blend in eggs, sour cream and vanilla; fold in chopped cookies. Spread mixture into prepared crust. Bake at 350°F 60 minutes or until set.

3. Cool on wire rack at room temperature. Refrigerate at least 4 hours. Halve remaining cookies; remove side of pan. To serve, garnish with whipped cream and cookie halves. *Makes 12 servings*

BEST WAYS TO AVOID CRACKS IN CHEESCAKE
The most common causes of cracks in cheesecakes are overbeating the batter, baking too long or in an oven that's too hot, or jarring the cake during baking or cooling.

Chocolatetown Special Cake

½ cup HERSHEY'S Cocoa or HERSHEY'S Dutch Processed Cocoa
½ cup boiling water
⅔ cup shortening
1¾ cups sugar
 1 teaspoon vanilla extract
 2 eggs
2¼ cups all-purpose flour
1½ teaspoons baking soda
½ teaspoon salt
1⅓ cups buttermilk or sour milk*
 One-Bowl Buttercream Frosting (recipe follows)

To sour milk: Use 4 teaspoons white vinegar plus milk to equal 1⅓ cups.

1. Heat oven to 350°F. Grease and flour two 9-inch round baking pans.

2. Stir together cocoa and water in small bowl until smooth. Beat shortening, sugar and vanilla in large bowl until fluffy. Add eggs; beat well. Stir together flour, baking soda and salt; add to shortening mixture alternately with buttermilk, beating until well blended. Add cocoa mixture; beat well. Pour batter into prepared pans.

3. Bake 35 to 40 minutes or until wooden pick inserted in center comes out clean. Cool 10 minutes; remove from pans to wire racks. Cool completely. Frost with One-Bowl Buttercream Frosting.

Makes 8 to 10 servings

One-Bowl Buttercream Frosting

 6 tablespoons butter or margarine, softened
2⅔ cups powdered sugar
 ½ cup HERSHEY'S Cocoa or HERSHEY'S Dutch Processed Cocoa
 4 to 6 tablespoons milk
 1 teaspoon vanilla extract

Beat butter in medium bowl. Add powdered sugar and cocoa alternately with milk, beating to spreading consistency. Stir in vanilla.

Makes about 2 cups frosting

Easy Fudge Pots de Crème

1 package (4-serving size) chocolate cook & serve pudding and pie filling mix*
2 cups half-and-half or whole milk
1 cup HERSHEY'S Semi-Sweet Chocolate Chips
Sweetened whipped cream
HERSHEY'S Cocoa (optional)

*Do not use instant pudding mix.

1. Stir together pudding mix and half-and-half in medium saucepan. Cook over medium heat, stirring constantly, until mixture comes to a full boil. Remove from heat.

2. Add chocolate chips; stir until chips are melted and mixture is smooth.

3. Spoon into demitasse cups or small dessert dishes. Press plastic wrap directly onto surface. Refrigerate several hours or until chilled. Garnish with whipped cream; sift cocoa over top, if desired.

Makes 8 servings

Creamy Chocolate Dipped Strawberries

1 cup HERSHEY'S Semi-Sweet Chocolate Chips
½ cup HERSHEY'S Premier White Chips
1 tablespoon shortening (do *not* use butter, margarine or oil)
Fresh strawberries, rinsed and patted dry (about 2 pints)

1. Line tray with wax paper.

2. Place chocolate chips, white chips and shortening in medium microwave-safe bowl. Microwave at HIGH (100%) 1 minute; stir. If necessary, microwave at HIGH an additional 15 seconds at a time, stirring after each heating, just until chips are melted when stirred. Holding top, dip bottom two-thirds of each strawberry into melted mixture; shake gently to remove excess. Place on prepared tray.

3. Refrigerate about 1 hour or until coating is firm. Cover; refrigerate leftover dipped berries. For best results, use within 24 hours.

Makes about 3 dozen dipped berries

German's® Sweet Chocolate Cake

1 package (4 ounces) BAKER'S® GERMAN'S® Sweet Baking
   Chocolate
½ cup water
2 cups flour
1 teaspoon baking soda
¼ teaspoon salt
1 cup (2 sticks) butter or margarine, softened
2 cups sugar
4 egg yolks
1 teaspoon vanilla
1 cup buttermilk
4 egg whites
   Baker's® Coconut-Pecan Filling and Frosting (recipe page 162)

HEAT oven to 350°F. Line bottoms of three 9-inch layer pans with waxed paper.

MICROWAVE chocolate and water in large microwavable bowl on HIGH 1½ to 2 minutes or until chocolate is almost melted, stirring halfway through heating time. Stir until chocolate is completely melted.

MIX flour, baking soda and salt; set aside. Beat butter and sugar in large bowl with electric mixer until light and fluffy. Add egg yolks, one at a time, beating well after each addition. Stir in chocolate and vanilla. Add flour mixture alternately with buttermilk, beating after each addition until smooth.

BEAT egg whites in another large bowl with electric mixer on high speed until stiff peaks form. Gently stir into batter. Pour batter into prepared pans.

BAKE for 30 minutes or until cake springs back when lightly touched in center.

continued on page 162

German's® Sweet Chocolate Cake, continued

REMOVE from oven; immediately run spatula between cakes and sides of pans. Cool in pans 15 minutes. Remove from pans; peel off waxed paper. Cool on wire racks.

SPREAD Classic Coconut-Pecan Filling and Frosting between layers and over top of cake.   *Makes 12 servings*

Note: This delicate cake will have a flat, slightly sugary top crust that tends to crack. This is normal and the frosting will cover it up.

Prep: 30 minutes
Bake: 30 minutes

Coconut-Pecan Filling and Frosting

   1 can (12 ounces) evaporated milk
1½ cups sugar
  ¾ cup (1½ sticks) butter or margarine
   4 egg yolks, slightly beaten
1½ teaspoons vanilla
   1 package (7 ounces) BAKER'S® ANGEL FLAKE® Coconut (2⅔ cups)
1½ cups chopped pecans

STIR milk, sugar, butter, egg yolks and vanilla in saucepan. Cook on medium heat 12 minutes or until thickened and golden brown, stirring constantly. Remove from heat.

STIR in coconut and pecans. Cool to room temperature and spreading consistency.   *Makes about 4½ cups*

Kahlúa® Chocolate-Mint Trifle

1 chocolate cake mix (without pudding)
1 cup KAHLÚA® Liqueur
2 boxes (4-serving size) instant chocolate pudding mix
3½ cups milk
3 cups whipped topping
Peppermint candy, crushed

Prepare, bake and cool cake in 13×9-inch baking pan according to package directions. Poke holes in cake with fork; pour Kahlúa® over top. Refrigerate overnight. Cut cake into cubes.

Prepare pudding mix with milk in large bowl according to package directions. Layer in large clear glass trifle dish or glass bowl ⅓ each of cake cubes, pudding, whipped topping and candy. Repeat layers two more times. Refrigerate leftovers.   *Makes about 18 servings*

Chocolate Almond Biscotti

- **1 package DUNCAN HINES® Moist Deluxe® Dark Chocolate Cake Mix**
- **1 cup all-purpose flour**
- **½ cup (1 stick) butter or margarine, melted**
- **2 eggs**
- **1 teaspoon almond extract**
- **½ cup chopped almonds**
- **White chocolate, melted (optional)**

Preheat oven to 350°F. Line 2 baking sheets with parchment paper.

Combine cake mix, flour, butter, eggs and almond extract in large bowl. Beat at low speed with electric mixer until well blended; stir in nuts. Divide dough in half. Shape each half into a 12×2-inch log; place logs on prepared baking sheets. (Bake logs separately.)

Bake 30 to 35 minutes or until toothpick inserted in center comes out clean. Remove logs from oven; cool on baking sheets 15 minutes. Using serrated knife, cut logs into ½-inch slices. Arrange slices on baking sheets. Bake biscotti 10 minutes. Remove to cooling racks; cool completely.

Dip one end of each biscotti in melted white chocolate, if desired. Allow white chocolate to set at room temperature before storing biscotti in airtight container.

Makes about 2½ dozen cookies

164

Original Nestlé® Toll House® Chocolate Chip Cookies

2¼ cups all-purpose flour
1 teaspoon baking soda
1 teaspoon salt
1 cup (2 sticks) butter or margarine, softened
¾ cup granulated sugar
¾ cup packed brown sugar
1 teaspoon vanilla extract
2 large eggs
2 cups (12-ounce package) NESTLÉ® TOLL HOUSE® Semi-Sweet Chocolate Morsels
1 cup chopped nuts

PREHEAT oven to 375°F.

COMBINE flour, baking soda and salt in small bowl. Beat butter, granulated sugar, brown sugar and vanilla extract in large mixer bowl until creamy. Add eggs, one at a time, beating well after each addition. Gradually beat in flour mixture. Stir in morsels and nuts. Drop by rounded tablespoonfuls onto ungreased baking sheets.

BAKE for 9 to 11 minutes or until golden brown. Cool on baking sheets for 2 minutes; remove to wire racks to cool completely.

Makes about 5 dozen cookies

Pan Cookie Variation: **GREASE** 15×10-inch jelly-roll pan. Prepare dough as above. Spread into prepared pan. Bake for 20 to 25 minutes or until golden brown. Cool in pan on wire rack. Makes 4 dozen bars.

Original Nestlé® Toll House®
Chocolate Chip Cookies

Quick & Easy Fudgey Brownies

4 bars (1 ounce each) HERSHEY'S Unsweetened Baking Chocolate, broken into pieces
¾ cup (1½ sticks) butter or margarine
2 cups sugar
3 eggs
1½ teaspoons vanilla extract
1 cup all-purpose flour
1 cup chopped nuts (optional)
Creamy Quick Chocolate Frosting (recipe follows, optional)

1. Heat oven to 350°F. Grease 13×9×2-inch baking pan.

2. Place chocolate and butter in large microwave-safe bowl. Microwave at HIGH (100%) 1½ to 2 minutes or until chocolate is melted and mixture is smooth when stirred. Add sugar; stir with spoon until well blended. Add eggs and vanilla; mix well. Add flour and nuts, if desired; stir until well blended. Spread into prepared pan.

3. Bake 30 to 35 minutes or until wooden pick inserted in center comes out almost clean. Cool in pan on wire rack.

4. Frost with Creamy Quick Chocolate Frosting, if desired. Cut into squares. *Makes about 24 brownies*

Creamy Quick Chocolate Frosting

3 tablespoons butter or margarine
3 bars (1 ounce each) HERSHEY'S Unsweetened Baking Chocolate, broken into pieces
3 cups powdered sugar
½ cup milk
1 teaspoon vanilla extract
⅛ teaspoon salt

Melt butter and chocolate in saucepan over very low heat. Cook, stirring constantly, until chocolate is melted and mixture is smooth. Pour into large bowl; add powdered sugar, milk, vanilla and salt. Beat on medium speed of mixer until well blended. If necessary, refrigerate 10 minutes before spreading. *Makes about 2 cups frosting*

Gaiety Pastel Cookies

3½ cups flour
  1 teaspoon CALUMET® Baking Powder
1½ cups (3 sticks) butter or margarine
  1 cup sugar
  1 package (4-serving size) JELL-O® Brand Gelatin Dessert, any
    flavor*
  1 egg
  1 teaspoon vanilla
    Additional JELL-O® Brand Gelatin Dessert, any flavor*

*For best results, use same flavor.

HEAT oven to 400°F.

MIX flour and baking powder in medium bowl. Beat butter in large bowl with electric mixer to soften. Gradually add sugar and 1 package gelatin, beating until light and fluffy. Beat in egg and vanilla. Gradually add flour mixture, beating well after each addition.

SHAPE dough into 1-inch balls. Place on ungreased cookie sheets. Flatten with bottom of glass. Sprinkle with additional gelatin.

BAKE 10 to 12 minutes or until edges are lightly browned. Remove from cookie sheets. Cool on wire racks. Store in tightly covered container.   *Makes about 5 dozen cookies*

Prep Time: 40 minutes
Bake Time: 12 minutes

Oatmeal Cookies

1 cup all-purpose flour
1 teaspoon baking powder
½ teaspoon baking soda
½ teaspoon salt
¼ cup MOTT'S® Cinnamon Apple Sauce
2 tablespoons margarine
½ cup granulated sugar
½ cup firmly packed light brown sugar
1 egg or ¼ cup egg substitute
1 teaspoon vanilla extract
1⅓ cups uncooked rolled oats
½ cup raisins (optional)

1. Heat oven to 375°F. Lightly spray cookie sheet with cooking spray. In large bowl, mix flour, baking powder, baking soda and salt. In separate bowl, beat together apple sauce, margarine, granulated and brown sugars, egg, and vanilla until margarine forms pea-sized pieces. Add flour mixture to apple sauce mixture. Mix well. Fold in oats and raisins. Drop rounded teaspoonfuls onto cookie sheet; bake 5 minutes. Remove cookies from cookie sheet and cool completely on wire rack.

Makes 36 cookies

Top to bottom: Oatmeal Cookies
and Gingersnaps (page 176)

Chocolate Chunk Caramel Pecan Brownies

4 squares BAKER'S® Unsweetened Baking Chocolate
¾ cup (1½ sticks) butter or margarine
2 cups sugar
4 eggs
1 cup flour
1 package (14 ounces) KRAFT® Caramels, unwrapped
⅓ cup whipping (heavy) cream
2 cups pecan or walnut halves, divided
1 package (12 ounces) BAKER'S® Semi-Sweet Chocolate Chunks, divided

HEAT oven to 350°F. Line 13×9-inch baking pan with foil; grease foil.

MICROWAVE chocolate and butter in large microwavable bowl on HIGH 2 minutes or until butter is melted. Stir until chocolate is completely melted. Stir sugar into chocolate mixture until well blended. Mix in eggs. Stir in flour until well blended. Spread ½ of brownie batter in prepared pan.

BAKE 25 minutes or until brownie is firm to the touch.

MEANWHILE, microwave caramels and cream in microwavable bowl on HIGH 2 minutes or until caramels begin to melt. Stir until smooth. Stir in 1 cup of pecan halves. Gently spread caramel mixture over baked brownie in pan. Sprinkle with ½ of chocolate chunks. Pour remaining unbaked brownie batter evenly over top; sprinkle with remaining chocolate chunks and 1 cup pecan halves. (Some caramel mixture may peak through.)

BAKE an additional 30 minutes or until brownie is firm to the touch. Cool in pan on wire rack. Lift out of pan onto cutting board.

Makes 2 dozen brownies

Tip: For 13×9-inch glass baking dish, bake at 325°F.

Prep Time: 20 minutes
Bake Time: 55 minutes

Gingersnaps

2½ cups all-purpose flour
1½ teaspoons ground ginger
1 teaspoon baking soda
1 teaspoon ground allspice
½ teaspoon salt
1½ cups sugar
2 tablespoons margarine, softened
½ cup MOTT'S® Apple Sauce
¼ cup GRANDMA'S® Molasses

1. Preheat oven to 375°F. Spray cookie sheet with nonstick cooking spray.

2. In medium bowl, sift together flour, ginger, baking soda, allspice and salt.

3. In large bowl, beat sugar and margarine with electric mixer at medium speed until blended. Whisk in apple sauce and molasses.

4. Add flour mixture to apple sauce mixture; stir until well blended.

5. Drop rounded tablespoonfuls of dough 1 inch apart onto prepared cookie sheet. Flatten each slightly with moistened fingertips.

6. Bake 12 to 15 minutes or until firm. Cool completely on wire rack.

Makes 3 dozen cookies

Oatmeal Hermits

3 cups QUAKER® Oats (quick or old fashioned, uncooked)
1 cup all-purpose flour
1 cup (2 sticks) butter or margarine, melted
1 cup firmly packed brown sugar
1 cup raisins
½ cup chopped nuts
1 egg
¼ cup milk
1 teaspoon vanilla
1 teaspoon ground cinnamon
½ teaspoon baking soda
½ teaspoon salt (optional)
¼ teaspoon ground nutmeg

Heat oven to 375°F. In large bowl, combine all ingredients; mix well. Drop by rounded tablespoonfuls onto ungreased cookie sheets. Bake 8 to 10 minutes. Cool 1 minute on cookie sheets; remove to wire cooling rack.   *Makes about 3 dozen*

For Bar Cookies: Press dough into ungreased 15×10-inch jelly-roll pan. Bake about 17 minutes or until golden brown. Cool completely; cut into bars.

BEST WAY TO COOL COOKIES
Remove cookies with a spatula and place on a wire rack to cool. If cookies seem too tender or start to fall apart, allow them to cool for a few minutes on the cookie sheet before transferring.

177

Ultimate Sugar Cookies

COOKIES

1¼ cups granulated sugar

1 Butter Flavor CRISCO® Stick or 1 cup Butter Flavor CRISCO® all-vegetable shortening

2 eggs

¼ cup light corn syrup or regular pancake syrup

1 tablespoon vanilla

3 cups all-purpose flour plus 4 tablespoons, divided

¾ teaspoon baking powder

½ teaspoon baking soda

½ teaspoon salt

Decorations of your choice: colored sugar crystals, frosting, decors, candies, chips, nuts, raisins, decorating gel

1. Combine sugar and 1 cup shortening in large bowl. Beat at medium speed of electric mixer until well blended. Add eggs, syrup and vanilla. Beat until well blended and fluffy.

2. Combine 3 cups flour, baking powder, baking soda and salt. Add gradually to creamed mixture at low speed. Mix until well blended. Divide dough into 4 quarters. If dough is too soft to roll, wrap with plastic wrap. Refrigerate 1 hour.

3. Heat oven to 375°F. Place sheets of foil on countertop.

4. Spread 1 tablespoon flour on large sheet of waxed paper. Place one fourth of dough on floured paper. Flatten slightly with hands. Turn dough over and cover with another large sheet of waxed paper. Roll dough to ¼-inch thickness. Remove top sheet of waxed paper.

5. Cut out cookies with floured cutter. Transfer to ungreased baking sheet with large pancake turner. Place 2 inches apart. Roll out remaining dough. Sprinkle with granulated sugar, colored sugar crystals, decors or leave plain to frost or decorate when cooled.

6. Bake one baking sheet at a time at 375°F for 5 to 9 minutes, depending on the size of your cookies. (Bake smaller, thinner cookies closer to 5 minutes; larger cookies closer to 9 minutes.) *Do not overbake.* Cool 2 minutes on baking sheet. Remove cookies to foil to cool completely, frost if desired. *Makes about 3 to 4 dozen cookies*

Chocolate Marbled Blondies

½ cup (1 stick) butter or margarine, softened
½ cup firmly packed light brown sugar
1 large egg
2 teaspoons vanilla extract
1½ cups all-purpose flour
1¼ teaspoons baking soda
1 cup "M&M's"® Chocolate Mini Baking Bits, divided
4 ounces cream cheese, softened
2 tablespoons granulated sugar
1 large egg yolk
¼ cup unsweetened cocoa powder

Preheat oven to 350°F. Lightly grease 9×9×2-inch baking pan; set aside. In large bowl cream butter and brown sugar until light and fluffy; beat in egg and vanilla. In medium bowl combine flour and baking soda; blend into creamed mixture. Stir in ⅔ cup "M&M's"® Chocolate Mini Baking Bits; set aside. Dough will be stiff. In separate bowl beat together cream cheese, granulated sugar and egg yolk until smooth; stir in cocoa powder until well blended. Place chocolate-cheese mixture in six equal portions evenly onto bottom of prepared pan. Place reserved dough around cheese mixture and swirl slightly with tines of fork. Pat down evenly on top. Sprinkle with remaining ⅓ cup "M&M's"® Chocolate Mini Baking Bits. Bake 25 to 30 minutes or until toothpick inserted in center comes out with moist crumbs. Cool completely. Cut into bars. Store in refrigerator in tightly covered container. *Makes 16 bars*

Chocolate-Peanut Butter Checkerboards

½ **cup (1 stick) butter or margarine, softened**
1 **cup sugar**
1 **egg**
1 **teaspoon vanilla extract**
1 **cup plus 3 tablespoons all-purpose flour, divided**
½ **teaspoon baking soda**
¼ **cup HERSHEY:S Cocoa**
½ **cup REESE'S® Peanut Butter Chips**

1. Beat butter, sugar, egg and vanilla in large bowl until fluffy. Add 1 cup flour and baking soda; beat until blended. Remove ¾ cup batter to small bowl; set aside. Add cocoa and remaining 3 tablespoons flour to remaining batter in large bowl; blend well.

2. Place peanut butter chips in small microwave-safe bowl. Microwave at HIGH (100%) 30 seconds or until melted and smooth when stirred. Immediately add to batter in small bowl, stirring until smooth. Divide chocolate dough into four equal parts. Roll each part between plastic wrap or waxed paper into a log 7 inches long about 1 inch in diameter. Repeat with peanut butter dough. Wrap the eight rolls individually in waxed paper or plastic wrap. Refrigerate several hours until very firm.

3. Heat oven to 350°F. Remove rolls from waxed paper. Place 1 chocolate roll and 1 peanut butter roll side by side on a cutting board. Top each roll with another roll of the opposite flavor to make checkerboard pattern. Lightly press rolls together; repeat with remaining four rolls. Working with one checkerboard at a time (keep remaining checkerboard covered and refrigerated), cut into ¼-inch slices. Place on ungreased cookie sheet.

4. Bake 8 to 9 minutes or until peanut butter portion is lightly browned. Cool 1 minute; remove from cookie sheet to wire rack. Cool completely. *Makes about 4½ dozen cookies*

Chocolate Macadamia Crunch

**1 Butter Flavor CRISCO® Stick or 1 cup Butter Flavor CRISCO®
all-vegetable shortening plus additional for greasing**
¾ cup granulated sugar
½ cup firmly packed dark brown sugar
2 eggs
2 tablespoons buttermilk
2 teaspoons vanilla
1½ cups all-purpose flour
½ cup oats (old-fashioned, uncooked)
1 teaspoon baking soda
½ teaspoon salt
2 cups milk chocolate chips
1 cup coarsely chopped macadamia nuts

1. Combine shortening, granulated sugar, brown sugar, eggs, buttermilk and vanilla in large bowl. Beat at medium speed of electric mixer until light and fluffy.

2. Combine flour, oats, baking soda and salt. Add gradually to creamed mixture at low speed. Beat until well blended. Stir in chocolate chips and nuts with spoon. Cover. Refrigerate at least 30 minutes.

3. Heat oven to 325°F. Grease baking sheet with shortening. Place sheets of foil on countertop for cooling cookies.

4. Drop dough by tablespoonfuls 3 inches apart onto greased baking sheet.

5. Bake at 325°F for 14 to 16 minutes or until light golden brown. *Do not overbake.* Cool 2 minutes on baking sheet. Remove cookies to foil to cool completely. *Makes about 2½ dozen cookies*

Fudgy Hazelnut Brownies

1 (21-ounce) package DUNCAN HINES® Chewy Fudge Brownie Mix
2 eggs
½ cup vegetable oil
¼ cup water
1 cup chopped toasted hazelnuts
1 cup semisweet chocolate chips
1 cup DUNCAN HINES® Dark Chocolate Frosting
3 squares white chocolate, melted

Preheat oven to 350°F. Grease bottom only of 13×9-inch baking pan.

Combine brownie mix, eggs, oil and water in large bowl. Stir with spoon until well blended, about 50 strokes. Stir in nuts and chips. Spoon into prepared pan. Bake 25 to 30 minutes or until set. Cool completely.

Heat frosting in microwave oven at HIGH for 15 seconds or until thin; stir well. Spread over brownies. Spoon dollops of white chocolate over chocolate frosting; marble white chocolate through frosting. Cool completely. Cut into bars.   *Makes 24 brownies*

BEST WAY TO CUT BROWNIES
For easy removal of brownies (and no cleanup!), line the baking pan with foil and leave at least 3 inches hanging over each end. Use the foil to lift out the treats, place them on a cutting board and carefully remove the foil. Then simply cut them into pieces.

Colorific Chocolate Chip Cookies

- 1 cup (2 sticks) butter or margarine, softened
- ⅔ cup granulated sugar
- ½ cup firmly packed light brown sugar
- 1 large egg
- 1 teaspoon vanilla extract
- 2 cups all-purpose flour
- ¾ teaspoon baking soda
- ¾ teaspoon salt
- 1¾ cups "M&M's"® Semi-Sweet Chocolate Mini Baking Bits
- ¾ cup chopped nuts, optional

Preheat oven to 375°F. In large bowl cream butter and sugars until light and fluffy; beat in egg and vanilla. In medium bowl combine flour, baking soda and salt; blend into creamed mixture. Stir in "M&M's"® Semi-Sweet Chocolate Mini Baking Bits and nuts, if desired. Drop by heaping tablespoonfuls about 2 inches apart onto ungreased cookie sheets. Bake 9 to 12 minutes or until lightly browned. Cool 1 minute on cookie sheets; cool completely on wire racks. Store in tightly covered container. *Makes about 3 dozen cookies*

Hint: For chewy cookies bake 9 to 10 minutes; for crispy cookies bake 11 to 12 minutes.

Pan Cookie Variation: Prepare dough as directed; spread into lightly greased 15×10×1-inch jelly-roll pan. Bake at 375°F for 18 to 22 minutes. Cool completely before cutting into 35 (2-inch) squares. For a more festive look, reserve ½ cup baking bits to sprinkle on top of dough before baking.

Best-Ever Short Cake

        2 cups all-purpose flour
        2 tablespoons sugar
        1 tablespoon baking powder
        1 teaspoon salt
        ¾ cup shortening
        1 cup milk
        2 boxes (10 ounces each) BIRDS EYE® frozen
            Strawberries, thawed
        Whipped topping (optional)

• Preheat oven to 450°F. Combine flour, sugar, baking powder and salt.

• Cut shortening into flour mixture until mixture resembles coarse cornmeal.

• Blend in milk; mix well. Spread dough in 9×9-inch baking pan.

• Bake 15 minutes. Serve warm or let cool; top with strawberries before serving. Garnish with whipped topping, if desired.   *Makes 6 to 9 servings*

Prep Time: 5 minutes
Cook Time: 15 minutes

190

Country Apple Rhubarb Pie

CRUST
> **9-inch Classic CRISCO® Double Crust (recipe page 202)**

FILLING
> **9 cups sliced peeled Granny Smith apples (about 3 pounds or**
>> **6 large apples)**
> **1½ cups chopped (about ½-inch pieces) fresh rhubarb, peeled if tough**
> **¾ cup granulated sugar**
> **½ cup firmly packed light brown sugar**
> **2 tablespoons all-purpose flour**
> **1 tablespoon cornstarch**
> **1 teaspoon ground cinnamon**
> **¼ teaspoon freshly grated nutmeg**

GLAZE
> **1 egg, beaten**
> **1 tablespoon water**
> **1 tablespoon granulated sugar**
> **1 teaspoon ground pecans or walnuts**
> **⅛ teaspoon ground cinnamon**

1. For crust, prepare dough. Roll and press bottom crust into 9- or 9½-inch deep-dish pie plate. *Do not bake.* Heat oven to 425°F.

2. For filling, combine apples and rhubarb in large bowl. Combine ¾ cup granulated sugar, brown sugar, flour, cornstarch, 1 teaspoon cinnamon and nutmeg in medium bowl. Sprinkle over fruit. Toss to coat. Spoon into unbaked pie crust. Moisten pastry edge with water. Cover pie with lattice top, cutting strips 1 inch wide. Flute edge high.

3. For glaze, combine egg and water in small bowl. Brush over crust. Combine remaining glaze ingredients in small bowl. Sprinkle over crust.

4. Bake at 425°F for 20 minutes. Reduce oven temperature to 350°F. Bake 30 to 40 minutes or until filling in center is bubbly and crust is golden brown. *Do not overbake.* Place sheet of foil or baking sheet under pie if it starts to bubble over. Cool to room temperature.
> *Makes one 9- or 9½-inch deep-dish pie (8 servings)*

Cranberry Cobbler

2 (16-ounce) cans sliced peaches in light syrup, drained
1 (16-ounce) can whole berry cranberry sauce
1 package DUNCAN HINES® Cinnamon Swirl Muffin Mix
½ cup chopped pecans
⅓ cup butter or margarine, melted
**   Whipped topping or ice cream**

Preheat oven to 350°F.

Cut peach slices in half lengthwise. Combine peach slices and cranberry sauce in *ungreased* 9-inch square pan. Knead swirl packet from Mix for 10 seconds. Squeeze contents evenly over fruit.

Combine muffin mix, contents of topping packet from mix and pecans in large bowl. Add melted butter. Stir until thoroughly blended (mixture will be crumbly). Sprinkle crumbs over fruit. Bake 40 to 45 minutes or until lightly browned and bubbly. Serve warm with whipped topping.   *Makes 9 servings*

Tip: Store leftovers in the refrigerator. Reheat in microwave oven to serve warm.

BEST TIP ON STORING PECANS
Pecans have a fat content of 70% (higher than most other nuts) so they are quite perishable. Shelled pecans can be stored in an airtight container up to 3 months in the refrigerator. For longer storage, up to 6 months, store in the freezer.

Philadelphia® 3-Step® Fruit Topped Cheesecake

2 packages (8 ounces each) PHILADELPHIA® Cream Cheese, softened
½ cup sugar
½ teaspoon vanilla
2 eggs
1 HONEY MAID® Graham Pie Crust (6 ounces)
2 cups fresh fruit slices
2 tablespoons strawberry or apple jelly, heated (optional)

1. **BEAT** cream cheese, sugar and vanilla with electric mixer on medium speed until well blended. Add eggs; mix just until blended.

2. **POUR** into crust.

3. **BAKE** at 350°F for 40 minutes or until center is almost set. Cool. Refrigerate 3 hours or overnight. Top with fruit; drizzle with jelly.

Makes 8 servings

Prep Time: 10 minutes plus refrigerating
Bake Time: 40 minutes

Crown Jewel Dessert

1 package (4-serving size) JELL-O® Brand Lime Flavor Gelatin
    Dessert*
1 package (4-serving size) JELL-O® Brand Orange Flavor Gelatin
    Dessert*
1 package (4-serving size) JELL-O® Brand Strawberry Flavor Gelatin
    Dessert*
3 cups boiling water
1½ cups cold water
1 cup boiling water
1 package (4-serving size) JELL-O® Brand Strawberry Flavor Gelatin
    Dessert
½ cup cold water
1 tub (8 ounces) COOL WHIP® Whipped Topping, thawed

Or use any 3 different flavors of JELL-O Brand Gelatin Dessert.

PREPARE lime, orange and 1 package strawberry gelatin separately as
directed on packages, using 1 cup boiling water and ½ cup cold water
for each. Pour each flavor into separate 8-inch square pans.
Refrigerate 4 hours or until firm. Cut into ½-inch cubes; measure
1½ cups of each flavor. (Use the remaining gelatin cubes for garnish if
desired or for snacking.)

STIR 1 cup boiling water into remaining package of strawberry gelatin
in medium bowl at least 2 minutes until completely dissolved. Stir in
½ cup cold water. Refrigerate 45 minutes or until slightly thickened
(consistency of unbeaten egg whites).

STIR in ½ of the whipped topping. Gently stir in measured gelatin
cubes. Pour into 9×5-inch loaf pan.

REFRIGERATE 4 hours or until firm. Unmold. Garnish with remaining
whipped topping and gelatin cubes, if desired.   *Makes 16 servings*

Prep Time: 45 minutes
Refrigerate Time: 8¾ hours

Classic Lemon Meringue Pie

CRUST
> **Classic CRISCO® Single Crust (recipe page 202)**

FILLING
- 1½ **cups sugar**
- ¼ **cup cornstarch**
- 3 **tablespoons all-purpose flour**
- ¼ **teaspoon salt**
- 1½ **cups hot water**
- 3 **egg yolks, beaten**
- 2 **tablespoons butter or margarine**
- 1½ **teaspoons grated lemon peel**
- ⅓ **cup plus 1 tablespoon fresh lemon juice**

MERINGUE
- ½ **cup sugar, divided**
- 1 **tablespoon cornstarch**
- ½ **cup cold water**
- 4 **egg whites**
- ¾ **teaspoon vanilla**

1. For crust, prepare and bake as directed. Cool. Heat oven to 350°F.

2. For filling, combine 1½ cups sugar, ¼ cup cornstarch, flour and salt in medium saucepan. Add 1½ cups hot water gradually, stirring constantly. Cook and stir on medium heat until mixture comes to a boil and thickens. Reduce heat to low. Cook and stir constantly 8 minutes. Remove from heat. Add about one third of hot mixture slowly to egg yolks. Mix well. Return mixture to saucepan. Bring mixture to a boil on medium-high heat. Reduce heat to low. Cook and stir 4 minutes. Remove from heat. Stir in butter and lemon peel. Add lemon juice slowly. Mix well. Spoon into baked pie crust.

3. For meringue, combine 2 tablespoons sugar, 1 tablespoon cornstarch and ½ cup cold water in small saucepan. Stir until cornstarch dissolves. Cook and stir on medium heat until mixture is clear. Cool.

continued on page 202

Classic Lemon Meringue Pie, continued

4. Combine egg whites and vanilla in large bowl. Beat at high speed of electric mixer until soft peaks form. Beat in remaining 6 tablespoons sugar, 1 tablespoon at a time. Beat well after each addition. Combine meringue with cornstarch mixture and continue beating until stiff peaks form. Spread over filling, covering completely and sealing to edge of pie.

5. Bake at 350°F for 12 to 15 minutes or until meringue is golden. *Do not overbake.* Cool to room temperature before serving. Refrigerate leftover pie.   *Makes 1 (9-inch) pie*

Classic Crisco® Crust

8-, 9- OR 10-INCH SINGLE CRUST
  1⅓ cups all-purpose flour
   ½ teaspoon salt
   ½ CRISCO® Stick or ½ cup CRISCO® Shortening
   3 tablespoons cold water

8- OR 9-INCH DOUBLE CRUST
   2 cups all-purpose flour
   1 teaspoon salt
   ¾ CRISCO® Stick or ¾ cup CRISCO® Shortening
   5 tablespoons cold water

1. Spoon flour into measuring cup and level. Combine flour and salt in medium bowl.

2. Cut in shortening using pastry blender (or 2 knives) until all flour is blended to form pea-size chunks.

3. Sprinkle with water, 1 tablespoon at a time. Toss lightly with fork until dough forms a ball.

FOR SINGLE CRUST PIES
1. Press dough between hands to form 5- to 6-inch "pancake." Flour rolling surface and rolling pin lightly. Roll dough into circle.

2. Trim 1 inch larger than upside-down pie plate. Loosen dough carefully.

3. Fold dough into quarters. Unfold and press into pie plate. Fold edge under. Flute.

FOR BAKED PIE CRUSTS

1. For recipes using baked pie crust, heat oven to 425°F. Prick bottom and side thoroughly with fork (50 times) to prevent shrinkage.

2. Bake at 425°F for 10 to 15 minutes or until lightly browned.

FOR UNBAKED PIE CRUSTS

1. For recipes using unbaked pie crust, follow baking directions given in each recipe.

FOR DOUBLE CRUST PIES

1. Divide dough in half. Roll each half separately. Transfer bottom crust to pie plate. Trim edge even with pie plate.

2. Add desired filling to unbaked pie crust. Moisten pastry edge with water. Lift top crust onto filled pie. Trim ½ inch beyond edge of pie plate. Fold top edge under bottom crust. Flute. Cut slits in top crust to allow steam to escape. Bake according to specific recipe directions.

BEST TIP FOR HANDLING PIE CRUST
If the dough is sticky and difficult to handle, refrigerate it until firm. Flour the rolling pin and surface just enough to prevent sticking. Handle the dough quickly and lightly. A tough pie crust is often the result of too much flour worked into the dough and overhandling it.

Rice Pudding

1¼ cups water, divided
½ cup uncooked long-grain rice
2 cups evaporated skim milk
½ cup granulated sugar
½ cup raisins
½ cup MOTT'S® Natural Apple Sauce
3 tablespoons cornstarch
1 teaspoon vanilla extract
   Brown sugar or nutmeg (optional)
   Fresh raspberries (optional)
   Orange peel strips (optional)

1. In medium saucepan, bring 1 cup water to a boil. Add rice. Reduce heat to low and simmer, covered, 20 minutes or until rice is tender and water is absorbed.

2. Add milk, granulated sugar, raisins and apple sauce. Bring to a boil. Reduce heat to low and simmer for 3 minutes, stirring occasionally.

3. Combine cornstarch and remaining ¼ cup water in small bowl. Stir into rice mixture. Simmer about 20 minutes or until mixture thickens, stirring occasionally. Remove from heat; stir in vanilla. Cool 15 to 20 minutes before serving. Sprinkle each serving with brown sugar or nutmeg and garnish with raspberries and orange peel, if desired. Refrigerate leftovers. *Makes 8 servings*

Creamy Cantaloupe

1 medium cantaloupe (about 3½ pounds)
¾ cup boiling water
1 package (4-serving size) JELL-O® Brand Gelatin, any flavor
½ cup cold orange juice
½ cup thawed COOL WHIP® Whipped Topping

CUT melon in half lengthwise; remove seeds. Scoop out melon, leaving about 1-inch thick border of melon. Dice scooped out melon. Drain well. Cut thin slice from bottom of each melon shell to allow shells to stand upright, or place in small bowls.

STIR boiling water into gelatin in large bowl at least 2 minutes until completely dissolved. Stir in cold juice. Refrigerate 15 minutes or until slightly thickened (consistency of unbeaten egg whites). Gently stir in whipped topping. Stir in reserved diced melon. Pour into melon shells.

REFRIGERATE 3 hours or until firm. Cut into wedges.

Makes 8 servings

Prep Time: 15 minutes
Refrigerate Time: 3 hours

BEST WAY TO CHOOSE A CANTALOUPE
Choose a cantaloupe that is firm but yields to gentle thumb pressure at the blossom end. The melon should have a pleasant odor. Ripen cantaloupe at room temperature; refrigerate it and be sure to use within 2 to 3 days.

Libby's® Famous Pumpkin Pie

- **¾ cup granulated sugar**
- **½ teaspoon salt**
- **1 teaspoon ground cinnamon**
- **½ teaspoon ground ginger**
- **¼ teaspoon ground cloves**
- **2 large eggs**
- **1 can (15 ounces) LIBBY'S® 100% Pure Pumpkin**
- **1 can (12 fluid ounces) NESTLÉ® CARNATION® Evaporated Milk***
- **1 *unbaked* 9-inch (4-cup volume) deep-dish pie shell**
  Whipped Cream

For lower fat/calorie pie, substitute CARNATION® Evaporated Lowfat Milk or Evaporated Fat Free Milk.

MIX sugar, salt, cinnamon, ginger and cloves in small bowl. Beat eggs in large bowl. Stir in pumpkin and sugar-spice mixture. Gradually stir in evaporated milk.

POUR into pie shell.

BAKE in preheated 425°F. oven for 15 minutes. Reduce temperature to 350°F.; bake 40 to 50 minutes or until knife inserted near center comes out clean. Cool on wire rack for 2 hours. Serve immediately or refrigerate. Top with whipped cream before serving.

Makes 8 servings

Note: Do not freeze, as this will cause the crust to separate from the filling.

Substitution: Substitute 1¾ teaspoons pumpkin pie spice for the cinnamon, ginger and cloves; however, the taste will be slightly different.

For 2 Shallow Pies: Substitute two 9-inch (2-cup volume) pie shells. Bake in preheated 425°F. oven for 15 minutes. Reduce temperature to 350°F.; bake for 20 to 30 minutes or until pies test done.

Cool 'n' Easy® Strawberry Pie

⅔ cup boiling water
1 package (4-serving size) JELL-O® Brand Strawberry Flavor Sugar
   Free Low Calorie Gelatin
½ cup cold water
   Ice cubes
1 tub (8 ounces) COOL WHIP LITE® Whipped Topping, thawed,
   divided
1 cup chopped strawberries
1 prepared reduced-fat graham cracker crumb crust (6 ounce or
   9 inch)
5 whole strawberries, halved

STIR boiling water into gelatin in large bowl at least 2 minutes until completely dissolved. Mix cold water and ice to make 1 cup. Add to gelatin, stirring until slightly thickened. Remove any remaining ice.

STIR in 2½ cups of the whipped topping with wire whisk until smooth. Mix in chopped strawberries. Refrigerate 15 to 20 minutes or until mixture is very thick and will mound. Spoon into crust.

REFRIGERATE 4 hours or overnight. Garnish with remaining whipped topping and strawberry halves. Store leftover pie in refrigerator.

Makes 8 servings

Prep Time: 10 minutes plus refrigerating

Baked Apple Crisp

8 cups thinly sliced unpeeled apples (about 8 medium)
2 tablespoons granulated sugar
4½ teaspoons lemon juice
4 teaspoons ground cinnamon, divided
1½ cups MOTT'S® Natural Apple Sauce
1 cup uncooked rolled oats
½ cup firmly packed light brown sugar
⅓ cup all-purpose flour
⅓ cup evaporated skimmed milk
¼ cup nonfat dry milk powder
1 cup vanilla nonfat yogurt

1. Preheat oven to 350°F. Spray 2-quart casserole dish with nonstick cooking spray.

2. In large bowl, toss apple slices with granulated sugar, lemon juice and 2 teaspoons cinnamon. Spoon into prepared dish. Spread apple sauce evenly over apple mixture.

3. In medium bowl, combine oats, brown sugar, flour, evaporated milk, dry milk powder and remaining 2 teaspoons cinnamon. Spread over apple sauce.

4. Bake 35 to 40 minutes or until lightly browned and bubbly. Cool slightly; serve warm. Top each serving with dollop of yogurt.

Makes 12 servings

Baked Apple Crisp

Pineapple Fruit Tart

¼ cup ground almonds (about 2 tablespoons whole almonds)
¼ cup butter or margarine, softened
¼ cup sugar
2 tablespoons milk
½ teaspoon almond extract
¾ cup all-purpose flour
2 packages (3 ounces each) cream cheese, softened
2 tablespoons sour cream
¼ cup apricot preserves, divided
1 teaspoon vanilla extract
1 can (15¼ ounces) DEL MONTE® Sliced Pineapple In Its Own Juice, drained and cut in halves
2 kiwifruits, peeled, sliced and cut into halves
1 cup sliced strawberries

1. Combine almonds, butter, sugar, milk and almond extract; mix well. Blend in flour. Chill dough 1 hour.

2. Press dough evenly onto bottom and up side of tart pan with removable bottom.

3. Bake at 350°F, 15 to 18 minutes or until golden brown. Cool.

4. Combine cream cheese, sour cream, 1 tablespoon apricot preserves and vanilla. Spread onto crust. Arrange pineapple, kiwi and strawberries over cream cheese mixture.

5. Heat remaining 3 tablespoons apricot preserves in small saucepan over low heat. Spoon over fruit. *Makes 8 servings*

Ritz® Mock Apple Pie

Pastry for two-crust 9-inch pie
36 RITZ® Crackers, coarsely broken (about 1¾ cups crumbs)
1¾ cups water
2 cups sugar
2 teaspoons cream of tartar
2 tablespoons lemon juice
Grated peel of 1 lemon
2 tablespoons margarine or butter
½ teaspoon ground cinnamon

1. Roll out half the pastry and line 9-inch pie plate. Place cracker crumbs in prepared crust; set aside.

2. Heat water, sugar and cream of tartar to a boil in saucepan over high heat; simmer 15 minutes. Add lemon juice and peel; cool. Pour syrup over cracker crumbs. Dot with margarine or butter; sprinkle with cinnamon. Roll out remaining pastry; place over pie. Trim, seal and flute edges. Slit top crust to allow steam to escape.

3. Bake at 425°F for 30 to 35 minutes or until crust is crisp and golden. Serve warm or let cool completely before serving.

Makes 10 servings

Baked Apples

2 tablespoons sugar
2 tablespoons GRANDMA'S® Molasses
2 tablespoons raisins, chopped
2 tablespoons chopped walnuts
6 apples, cored

Heat oven to 350°F. In medium bowl, combine sugar, molasses, raisins and walnuts. Fill apple cavities with molasses mixture. Place in 13×9-inch baking dish. Pour ½ cup hot water over the apples and bake 25 minutes or until soft.

Makes 6 servings

ACKNOWLEDGMENTS

The publisher would like to thank the companies and organizations listed below for the use of their recipes and photographs in this publication.

A.1.® Steak Sauce

Barilla America, Inc.

Birds Eye®

Bob Evans®

Butterball® Turkey Company

Clamato® is a registered trademark of Mott's, Inc.

COLLEGE INN® Broth

ConAgra Foods®

Del Monte Corporation

Dole Food Company, Inc.

Duncan Hines® and Moist Deluxe® are registered trademarks of Aurora Foods Inc.

Eagle® Brand

Filippo Berio® Olive Oil

Fleischmann's® Yeast

Grandma's® is a registered trademark of Mott's, Inc.

Grey Poupon® Dijon Mustard

Hebrew National®

Hershey Foods Corporation

Holland House® is a registered trademark of Mott's, Inc.

Hormel Foods, LLC

Kahlúa® Liqueur

The Kingsford Products Company

KNOX® Unflavored Gelatin

Kraft Foods Holdings

Lawry's® Foods, Inc.

© Mars, Incorporated 2002

McIlhenny Company (TABASCO® brand Pepper Sauce)

Mott's® is a registered trademark of Mott's, Inc.

Nestlé USA

OREO® Chocolate Sandwich Cookies

The Quaker® Oatmeal Kitchens

Reckitt Benckiser Inc.

RITZ® Crackers

Riviana Foods Inc.

The J.M. Smucker Company

StarKist® Seafood Company

Tyson Foods, Inc.

Uncle Ben's Inc.

Unilever Bestfoods North America

Veg-All®

217

METRIC CONVERSION CHART

VOLUME MEASUREMENTS (dry)

$^1/_8$ teaspoon = 0.5 mL
$^1/_4$ teaspoon = 1 mL
$^1/_2$ teaspoon = 2 mL
$^3/_4$ teaspoon = 4 mL
1 teaspoon = 5 mL
1 tablespoon = 15 mL
2 tablespoons = 30 mL
$^1/_4$ cup = 60 mL
$^1/_3$ cup = 75 mL
$^1/_2$ cup = 125 mL
$^2/_3$ cup = 150 mL
$^3/_4$ cup = 175 mL
1 cup = 250 mL
2 cups = 1 pint = 500 mL
3 cups = 750 mL
4 cups = 1 quart = 1 L

VOLUME MEASUREMENTS (fluid)

1 fluid ounce (2 tablespoons) = 30 mL
4 fluid ounces ($^1/_2$ cup) = 125 mL
8 fluid ounces (1 cup) = 250 mL
12 fluid ounces (1$^1/_2$ cups) = 375 mL
16 fluid ounces (2 cups) = 500 mL

WEIGHTS (mass)

$^1/_2$ ounce = 15 g
1 ounce = 30 g
3 ounces = 90 g
4 ounces = 120 g
8 ounces = 225 g
10 ounces = 285 g
12 ounces = 360 g
16 ounces = 1 pound = 450 g

DIMENSIONS

$^1/_{16}$ inch = 2 mm
$^1/_8$ inch = 3 mm
$^1/_4$ inch = 6 mm
$^1/_2$ inch = 1.5 cm
$^3/_4$ inch = 2 cm
1 inch = 2.5 cm

OVEN TEMPERATURES

250°F = 120°C
275°F = 140°C
300°F = 150°C
325°F = 160°C
350°F = 180°C
375°F = 190°C
400°F = 200°C
425°F = 220°C
450°F = 230°C

BAKING PAN SIZES

Utensil	Size in Inches/Quarts	Metric Volume	Size in Centimeters
Baking or Cake Pan (square or rectangular)	$8 \times 8 \times 2$	2 L	$20 \times 20 \times 5$
	$9 \times 9 \times 2$	2.5 L	$23 \times 23 \times 5$
	$12 \times 8 \times 2$	3 L	$30 \times 20 \times 5$
	$13 \times 9 \times 2$	3.5 L	$33 \times 23 \times 5$
Loaf Pan	$8 \times 4 \times 3$	1.5 L	$20 \times 10 \times 7$
	$9 \times 5 \times 3$	2 L	$23 \times 13 \times 7$
Round Layer Cake Pan	$8 \times 1^1/_2$	1.2 L	20×4
	$9 \times 1^1/_2$	1.5 L	23×4
Pie Plate	$8 \times 1^1/_4$	750 mL	20×3
	$9 \times 1^1/_4$	1 L	23×3
Baking Dish or Casserole	1 quart	1 L	—
	1$^1/_2$ quart	1.5 L	—
	2 quart	2 L	—